Transformative Worship

Transformative Worship

Changing Lives through Religious Experience

Laurene Beth Bowers

WIPF & STOCK · Eugene, Oregon

TRANSFORMATIVE WORSHIP
Changing Lives through Religious Experience

Copyright © 2017 Laurene Beth Bowers. All rights reserved. Except for brief quotations in critical publications or reviews, no part of this book may be reproduced in any manner without prior written permission from the publisher. Write: Permissions, Wipf and Stock Publishers, 199 W. 8th Ave., Suite 3, Eugene, OR 97401.

Wipf & Stock
An imprint of Wipf and Stock Publishers
199 W. 8th Ave., Suite 3
Eugene, OR 97401

www.wipfandstock.com

PAPERBACK ISBN: 978-1-5326-0606-9
HARDCOVER ISBN: 978-1-5326-0608-3
EBOOK ISBN: 978-1-5326-0607-6

Manufactured in the U.S.A.   JANUARY 26, 2017

To my husband,
Kent William Rhodehamel

Contents

Introduction | 1

Chapter 1   Three Cultural Shifts | 19
Chapter 2   The Church's Mission | 33
Chapter 3   The Function of Worship: Theological Reflection and Emotional Expression | 46
Chapter 4   Assessing Current Levels of Satisfaction | 58
Chapter 5   Interactive Worship: The Flow of Energy and Building Relationships | 74
Chapter 6   Faith Sharing and Formation: Witnessing, Small Groups, and Bible Study | 89
Chapter 7   New Rituals in Old Wineskins: Holy Days, Baptisms, Weddings, and Funerals | 105
Chapter 8   Music and the Diversity of Religious Needs | 116
Chapter 9   The Setting of Transformative Worship: Space, Time, and Imagination | 129
Chapter 10   Making Changes to Worship: Practical Ways to Deal with Resistance | 139

Bibliography | 153

Introduction

THE DAYS ARE GONE when people want to come to worship and sit passively in the pews and listen to a pastor preach a twenty-minute sermon.¹ Reading canned liturgy printed in a bulletin or projected onto a wide-screen lacks the inspirational liveliness they long to experience. Singing three hymns out of the same hymnal seems like singing "Rock of Ages" three times in the same worship service. When the offering plate is passed, they are unmoved to financially support an organization which doesn't seem to care about meeting their religious needs. From the perspective of many, including a growing number of boomers and Gen Xers, worship is a dreadfully boring ceremony, a monotonous ritual of repetition, irrelevant for daily living and disconnected from contemporary culture. Perhaps because of their parents' growing disinterest, most millennials have never set foot in a religious organization for any reason, including weddings, baptisms, and funerals.² Unless driven by a sense of family obligation to maintain affiliation with a beloved church, they are unlikely to wake up one Sunday morning and decide to attend worship.

What are people looking for from a religious organization? What does the church offer to change people's lives? How do we go about researching the answers to these questions? What if we identify what seekers are looking for but we (as members) don't want to offer it? Shouldn't we meet the needs of our faithful long-term members above the needs of those who have shown little or no interest in attending worship? Why doesn't another

---

1. With abiding love and deep respect, I acknowledge some are still satisfied with the way they worship.
2. See Reese, *Unbinding the Gospel*.

generation want to worship the same way we have always worshipped? What's wrong with the way we worship? What's the matter with people today that they don't feel compelled to belong to a church? What has changed in our cultural environment? How do we implement changes to the worship service and deal with the inevitable forces of resistance and even sabotage? How do we *not* let two or three people hold us hostage from moving forward to become the church we believe God is calling us to revitalize?

All efforts to numerically grow a congregation begin with two questions: what does our church have to offer seekers in our neighborhood and what are they looking for from a church? The wider apart the answer to these questions, the more likely a congregation is declining in its average worship attendance. The more similar the answers, the more likely the average attendance is increasing. Ideally, the answer is one and the same: what the congregation offers is what people in the community are seeking. Declining congregations don't tend to know what they have to offer *or* what people in the neighborhood are looking for. Instead, members hyper-focus on the decrease in worship attendance and the increase in other members becoming inactive, whether still in the pews or not. They complain how fewer members are doing more of the work while finances continue to dwindle. They may even be spending down their endowment just to keep the doors open.

This book is intended to help declining congregations discern what seekers are looking for so members can prayerfully decide if they are willing to change the way they worship to meet those needs.

As a church growth consultant, I set out on a soul-searching mission, a research project, a holy adventure of sorts, to discern emerging new trends in worship. I imagined what it must have been like to be one of Jesus's disciples, to decide what we would do when we came together to encourage each other as new Christians on the pilgrimage of forming and strengthening our faith. What reason would God have for calling us to be a new start if our church did not yet exist in our community? I prayed about whether we still need organized religion today, especially when so many people identify themselves as Christians yet have no church affiliation.[3] Is there a purpose to gathering together? To answer these questions and several others, I trekked on a four-year journey, visiting churches to attend worship in

---

3. Interestingly, Facebook asks for the user's religion and not their organizational affiliation.

Introduction

a variety of different contexts, from mainline to evangelical, mega to small group, historically-rooted to new church ministries.[4] I attended worship in churches with tall steeples and traditional architecture and those which met in store fronts, homes, cafes, and bars.

Surprisingly, I found little correlation between context and what I experienced as a meaningful encounter with God in Christ. I enjoyed worship while sitting on wooden benches under pine trees or sitting on beach chairs as the waves crashed upon the seashore. I enjoyed small group worship in the local bar where we indulged in libations and discussed matters relating to the meaning of life, what God is like, and why life is so darn difficult sometimes (known as "theology on tap"). Sitting on sofas in someone's living room doing Bible study and sharing what is going on in our lives and how we see God involved felt personal and authentic. Each setting offered something unique but was not a significant factor in sensing God's presence or for faith formation. Some settings were simply more conducive to theological conversation, collective prayer, spiritual meditation, and the liturgical arts. Other settings seemed less favorable to encounter the God in Christ I had experienced elsewhere.

I was lured a few times by a sign announcing "contemporary" or "alternative" worship held in traditional buildings. These designations have become code for conventional worship, which exchanges traditional hymns for '80s praise music and uses PowerPoint to enhance the visuals on a large screen. Sitting in a fellowship hall on metal folding chairs with fifteen other people as the pastor read scripture and offered an improvised message did not feel any more spiritual than sitting upstairs in the sanctuary during the traditional worship service. In most instances, I got the feeling that these fifteen people were willing to support the pastor's efforts to numerically grow the congregation by showing up, but I suspected they, too, sensed something missing by worshipping God in the basement.[5] I noted that contemporary worship attracts the boomer generation, especially if the service incorporates praise music.[6] When I talked with millennials in their twenties and thirties, they told me that they like the more traditional music and prefer to worship in the sanctuary.

---

4. I expected I would find new trends to experience God in some of our new church starts but they seemed to replicate the status quo styles of the established church.

5. In many churches, the only one who really cares about church growth is the pastor.

6. Reflecting back on the contemporary worship movement, I now realize that it was an attempt to jazz up the worship for the current membership who could not admit they were bored with traditional worship.

During coffee hour after traditional worship, I asked members if they had ever attended the contemporary service. A frequent response was, "No, because I don't think we are here to be entertained." But if one thinks about it, traditional worship more closely resembles the performance mode of entertainment than most forms of contemporary worship. Worshippers receive a bulletin/program upon entering as a greeter/usher shows them to their seat.[7] When a worship leader/performer does something well or the congregation/audience agrees with what is being said, they applaud as a sign of affirmation. The worshipper/attendee is expected to remain otherwise idle and quiet (but can whisper softly). Like going to the movies, a Broadway show or the theatre, it doesn't matter who is sitting next to you as your gaze is directed toward the chancel/stage. The energy flows in one direction from the worship leaders/performers to the congregation/ticket holders.

I experienced out-of-the-box worship at the mega-churches (which I had heard so much about living in central Pennsylvania). I describe their style of worship as informal and breathe a sigh of relief I can wear jeans and not feel out of place. The music is upbeat and when I heard, "Heaven Let Your Light Shine Down" by Collective Soul, I wondered if I could come back next Sunday. It did take me a while (maybe twenty minutes) to realize the pastor was not physically present but was a high-tech hologram preaching from another campus (really?). They emphasize Bible literacy and offer opportunities for small group discussion. Even though I disagree with some of the theology touted at the mega-churches, I was impressed by their ability to clearly articulate their beliefs and how those beliefs inform their political/social/moral stances. Mainline members perceive that the mega-churches "tell people what to think," but I sensed their leaders were merely voicing where they are coming from concerning the issues of the day.[8]

I asked around in coffee shops and cafes if people went to church and if so, I inquired about their experiences of worship. Some eagerly spoke with me while others picked up their coffee cups and moved to another table. I realized I had to initiate a conversation by saying, "I'm not on a mission to convert anybody. I'm just a professor of religion doing research."[9]

---

7. When I asked young people why they thought churches use bulletins for their worship, the most common response was, "so that you can see how much longer this is going to last." What does that say about the way we worship?

8. Mainline members tend to perceive that mega-churches take this approach to converting seekers to Christianity.

9. I am also adjunct professor of religion at Dickinson College.

Introduction

This gave me some credibility that I did not have as a pastor or consultant. Most people were willing to talk to a researcher as long as I came across as curious and nonjudgmental. I met a few people who vehemently (and sometimes viciously) defended their church and its ideology (as if under attack by cultural forces of which I was personally responsible for sending their way). Occasionally, I came across someone who was enthusiastic about worship in a mainline church (and most often they talked about the music program). But the vast majority had not attended worship in years (if at all) and had little (if any) interest in discussing this subject matter.

I came across some churches while driving by and seeing something eye-catching (e.g., a name, an event, or a picturesque landscape). Others, I found by Googling the name of a community and the word "church." By doing this I learned something about the connection between the two and then I went on their website. What they say about themselves on the website should be confirmed by a web search (e.g., engaging in social justice or offering invitational events). For instance, if their website said they were committed to feeding the hungry or housing the homeless, I expected to see some evidence elsewhere on the web. I tried to verify that what they talk about in worship translates into Christian practice beyond the sanctuary walls. A lot of churches talk about advocating for the rights of the oppressed, but too often I couldn't find any evidence of their actually doing so in the community. If a church had almost no mention of itself beyond its own website, I wondered if they were too busy boasting about their ministries or just promoting wishful thinking about what they *should be* doing.

I discovered that many websites use similar designs and graphics in their construction. Initially, I assumed they all used the same company and were unaware of these similarities, but I later realized that this was an intentional result of "denominational branding." Several websites said the same thing, using the same tagline from their denomination with the attempt to distinguish themselves from other mainline denominations. Catchy phrases didn't inspire me to want to learn more about the church.[10] Prepackaged designs suggest a lack of effort to be creative and innovative. When I assumed that the designer of the website only had to insert the name of the church in its proper place, I wondered how much effort they were willing to invest in reaching new people.

---

10. For instance, the United Church of Christ quotes Gracie Allen, "Never put a period where God has put a comma."

The first screen of the website, its color, "wow" factor, message, and modern design all factored to spark or lose my interest. Within about five seconds I decided whether to click the X in the right hand corner and close the site. If the first screen had pictures of a lot of people I didn't know, I immediately clicked the X. Anything having to do with the maintenance of the organization (e.g., announcing a potluck dinner for next week or an upcoming meeting for the trustees) made me click the X. If the focus was on the building, the pastor's sermons, a request for money to repair the organ, click the X. A few websites intrigued me because they let visitors know what to wear, what not to wear, what was expected from members, worship etiquette, what they believed (condensed into a few sentences), and the process by which they go about discerning what they believe. This information made me feel like they anticipated (and wanted) visitors.[11]

Some websites feature profile pictures of recent visitors who gave a testimony of their experience of the worship service. Several spoke of how they weren't sure what they believed or how to put it together, but they intended to return the following Sunday to continue the process of discernment. Interestingly, no one mentioned returning because they liked the pastor and his or her style of preaching, the music, or because they thought the members were "warm and friendly."[12] Rather, their testimonials focused (almost exclusively) on their curiosity to be among those who believe in "something." I read these words on one website: "I don't know if I believe in Jesus, but I could tell these worshippers believe in him." Those browsing the website could also note when worshippers were open to talking about their faith and how they came to believe in what they believe. Another testimonial said, "This church respects that everyone isn't at the same place on their spiritual journey."[13]

When I pulled into the parking lot, it was nice to be greeted by a millennial waving hello and directing me where to park. If it was raining and

11. A few websites had a tab for visitors to ask questions via text or email. Their initial questions could be answered before walking through the door. I observed that the more a website was geared toward expecting visitors, the more visitors attended the worship service. Just as often, I observed that websites with information for members only attracted few, if any, visitors.

12. These are the assumptions churched people make for why seekers might return a second Sunday.

13. Given these statements, seeker-friendly worship is counterproductive to conversion. People who do not believe in Jesus are surrounded by others who also do not believe in Jesus, and no one ends up believing in Jesus. Transformative worship equips those who believe in Jesus to share with seekers what difference a relationship with him makes in their lives.

Introduction

I didn't have an umbrella, some churches had a team of youth carrying umbrellas, running people back and forth from their car to the front door. The more cars in the parking lot, the more excited I was to see why everyone else was there.[14] Curb appeal added to the ambience as well as a well-landscaped ground with flowers along the path toward the entrance. Some churches had memorial or prayer gardens and while I did not physically sit on the bench, I liked the idea that I could if I wanted to. Shoveled sidewalks, signs directing me where to go (especially which door to enter as a locked door made me want to get into my car and drive away) and seasonal decorations (not too tacky) served as symbols that the members care about their church, each other, and those curious enough to show up for worship at their church on a Sunday morning.

I felt welcomed when I arrived and someone opened the front door for me and smiled and said "good morning." In several mega-churches, I was greeted by a millennial woman. In most mainline churches, I was greeted by an elderly man. Whatever the generation of the greeter, I assumed he or she represented the average age of the worshippers inside.[15] Some greeters attempted to initiate conversation. I was asked, "Are you new to the community?" which could be translated as "we only accept locals." "Are you visiting with us for the first time?" was often followed by someone affixing a sticker with my name onto my clothing announcing my newbie status. Some said, "We are really glad (relieved) you are here this morning," which made me wonder why and what they needed from me. Questions tended to increase my anxiety (and I was already anxious about being in a new place) rather than put me at ease. I just wanted in. I didn't want to have to answer a lot of questions about myself and what I was doing there.

Once inside the church building, I often had to meander to find the sanctuary. Whereas everyone else seemed to know which way to go, I found myself trying to recall what the outside of the building looked like so I could figure out if the sanctuary was likely to be up or down the stairs, to

---

14. Interestingly, the mainline church constructed their parking lots in the back of the church and members tend to enter through the back door. Churches with newly-constructed buildings tend to pave the parking lot in the front of the church. This is because we have learned that people often make decisions about which church to attend by the number of cars in the parking lot. Half-jokingly, I suggest renting cars on Sunday morning and parking them on the front lawn.

15. A few times, I was pleasantly surprised to find a diversity of cultural groupings among the worshipping community, but I also looked for people "like" me with respect to age and ethnicity.

the right or to the left. The further away the sanctuary, the more anxious I felt as I walked down a long hallway only to open a door to a closet (which really happened to me!). When I eventually reached the sanctuary, there was usually someone to guide me in, but by then, it was too late. (I needed this person at the front door to direct me *to* the sanctuary.) I don't need help trying to find a seat unless there is assigned seating. I felt welcomed when served coffee (as long as it was gourmet), even better when I could bring my coffee cup (and all my tech devices) with me into the sanctuary space. As long as people didn't frown when they saw me or look away in disgust, I didn't need to meet or be greeted by anyone. I was there to experience their worship service.

I came to realize I was thinking more like someone who was unchurched (and it doesn't take long to think this way). I was gaining a deeper appreciation for what it is like to walk into a church where you don't know anyone and you are unfamiliar with the culture of the setting, its norms and rituals. I felt the awkwardness, uncertainty, and anxiety of being a visitor. I felt welcomed when one or two people introduced themselves and asked if I had any questions or needed assistance. Beyond basic hospitality, there is way too much emphasis on an extravagant welcome (and most of our members can no longer tell the difference between being warm and friendly and *pouncing*). A few times a greeter sat with me, but I wondered if I was being monitored for good behavior. I didn't like being singled out as a visitor. In most churches, I was hoping that I could sneak in and out. But whatever you do, do not shine the spotlight on me when worship begins by announcing my arrival.[16]

Eventually, it dawned on me that I, too, was searching for something spiritual missing from traditional worship or at least the ways of worship familiar to me in mainline religion. The more I travelled on this journey, the more this need intensified (or the more aware I became of it). Initially, I couldn't figure out if I was having a crisis of faith, reexamining everything I had always believed about God and the universe, or simply looking for new ways to express what I believe (and the crisis was probably a little of both).[17] As I encountered a variety of new forms of worship, these experiences began to renew and strengthen my faith. Through fresh expressions

---

16. It made me feel like I was the long-awaited messiah who was coming to "save" their church by pledging and being nominated for every committee vacancy.

17. For a more in-depth sharing of my spiritual journey, see *The God Beyond Organized Religion*.

INTRODUCTION

and meaningful moments, I somehow felt more connected to God and to the people with whom I worshipped. The more I talked with those who were wrestling with this same angel of doubt, the more I understood I was not alone in my quest to want to change the way we worship God in Christ. Others were searching with me for a transformative experience that changes lives.

I had to move beyond the premise that there is a "right" way to worship, as if God is sitting in the heavens with an ear pushed to the clouds waiting to hear the glorious lyric from the "Rock of Ages" hymn, "let me hide myself in thee." Nothing in the Bible says God wants us to use a 1955 format of praise and worship. Nothing says we have to sing three hymns and collect an offering. Nothing says we have to worship on Sunday morning in massive buildings, costly to heat and sucking the last drop of our financial resources. I tried to be open to alternative forms of worship, especially when I anticipated I would not like them. Some forms made me feel awkward (especially those that involve physical movement like swaying my arms). Grand, convoluted theological jargon lost me (and I went to seminary!) and so I tended to tune out anything requiring a dictionary. Well-planned-out worship wasn't achieved by following a bulletin from one form to another, as is done in traditional worship, but by identifying those with a gift to help others feel spiritually connected to God in Jesus. I feel that connection through those who knew how to use their gifts for worship and still leave room for the work of the Holy Spirit.

I enjoyed worship that I would describe as "personal." When one or two people shared stories about how God intervened in their lives during a recent event (e.g., crisis, trauma, or tragedy), I could identify with their stories and relate to their experience. They also witnessed to the transformative nature of God's intervention, reminding me that being a Christian makes a difference in my life (as does attending worship). These worship leaders talked about their struggles and joys with passion and conviction. The underlying premise was, "God helped me this way and God will help you, too." These testimonials shined light on dark places where God seems to be absent and reassured us that God often works behind the scenes and in the margins. I left worship feeling hopeful God is acting in ways which I had not previously thought about or observed. I also developed a deeper appreciation that everyone has a heart-breaking story. These experiences made me more sensitive to everyone I interacted with during the week.

Transformative Worship

I attended worship with as few as fifteen and as many as thousands, and while most congregations worship with numbers somewhere in between, the number of people in the sanctuary didn't seem to matter to the worshippers. I did wonder why one church had so few and another had so many, but there seemed to be little or no correlation between the worshippers' experience of God in the worship space and the number of people present. I listened to a few great sermons preached to a handful of people and a few terrible sermons preached to the masses. Some worship leaders seemed to be *expecting* more people than came (evidenced by the amount of chairs set up) while others were expecting fewer and had to scramble at the last minute to set up more chairs to accommodate the overflow. How the pastor *responded* to this expectation and managed his or her anxiety when that expectation did not match the actual attendance set the tone for the mood of worship.[18]

One of my more significant insights had to do with the source of this transformation. Before this journey, I had assumed the experience of worship is primarily dependent upon the pastor and/or the worship leaders: the quality of their leadership, their competence and charisma for preaching and teaching, reading scripture and exegesis, and how well the choir sang the anthem and the musicians played their instruments. I thought it was the function of the leadership to inspire worshippers to believe in Jesus and to want to follow his teachings. But over time, I became increasingly aware of the extent to which my experience of worship is dependent on the experience of *other* worshippers. For instance, when they seemed bored (looking demurely at the clock in the back of the sanctuary), then I felt bored. When they were having such a great time they were hoping worship would continue for another few hours, then I was in a joyful mood. This insight prompted me to shift my focus from the pastor or worship leaders to the worshippers themselves and how they contribute to the religious experience.

I also made an effort to attend worship in a wide variety of churches, from denominationally affiliated to inter-denominational to independent (non-denominational). Unless the pastor mentioned something about the

---

18. When I visited a few churches and the attendance was lower than average because it was the Sunday after a holiday or because of the weather or whatever, some pastors felt they needed to comment on such (e.g., "everyone must be away this week") to let the visitors know that there are usually more people present. If I was measuring the number of people in worship as an indicator of transformative worship that would be useful information. It was more important to the pastor than it was to me.

Introduction

denomination or there was a banner visibly hanging with the name on it, it was difficult to tell the difference. Some were more agenda-driven than others, emphasizing their stance on social and political issues and investing a lot of energy in defining themselves on one end of an imaginary spectrum between liberal and conservative, mainline and evangelical.[19] Sociologists, however, are noting that these categories are becoming increasingly irrelevant, especially among millennials.[20] (The worshippers themselves don't care about these categories but the worship leaders are clinging to them as instruments to launch a crusade of their own "rightness" to attract new people.)

The style of preaching revealed a slight correlation with political and social stances. Almost every preacher preached as if his or her perspective is the "right" one and all others who disagreed are "wrong."[21] Some began with a theological question, cited biblical phrases and referred to creeds as justification for the sermon's conclusion. (Sometimes taking so long to get there that I forgot the question.) Others began with the answer and harped on that answer until it was ringing in our ears (like a tune you can't get out of your head). Still others asked questions relevant to the challenges of daily life, exploring an array of possible answers and then spoke of a spiritual experience that led them to choose one option over another. They did not imply that their answer was the only one. A few pastors helped the worshippers to frame questions and then pointed them in the direction of how to find answers. These differences reflected the extent to which the function of preaching was to persuade, inform, or equip the worshippers.

Regretfully, I heard a lot of talk about social justice, assisting those currently broke or in a difficult place emotionally but I did not hear a lot of talk about how to put these beliefs into practice *to actually help others*. There seemed to be a gap between what everyone believes and how those beliefs influence the behavior of Christians past the postlude. I was not invited to attend a protest rally or serve a community meal or visit those home-bound, sick, or imprisoned. I felt like the premise of the sermon was: "this is what we believe a good Christian should be doing when the opportunity presents itself," and "when that opportunity arises, we will be

---

19. Another challenge of this project was to be able to sit through a worship service where I disagreed with the theology of the preacher/pastor/worship leader. Sometimes I imagined myself standing up and objecting, but I was afraid that one of the ushers/bouncers might throw me out of there.
20. See Putman and Campbell, *American Grace*.
21. This was true in mainline churches as well.

prepared." If you really want to assess how worshippers practice the Golden Rule, watch how they behave when another car cuts them off when trying to get out of the church's parking lot. I also heard a lot of talk about being environmentally conscious, only to see everyone getting into their mega-sized SUVs. There is a reason why those who are "spiritual but not religious" think members of organized religion are hypocritical.

As our society becomes increasingly diverse, especially with respect to ethnicity, the emerging church will embrace a greater tolerance and appreciation for diverse theological orientations (e.g., concepts of god). There will be less emphasis on being "right" and more emphasis on all the options. The church needs to become more adept at acknowledging different perspectives, worldviews, and ideologies arising from diverse social locations, experiences, and cultural traditions. Instead of arguing positions of who is right and who is wrong (often decided through the cultural lens of the dominant) and convincing others of their rightness so everyone *appears* to think the same way and agree, the emerging church will respect diversity of perspective. What people believe about themselves, their god, and the world around them reflects their experiences, from personal crises to traumatic events afflicting a cultural grouping.[22]

In this light, I recognize that what I think constitutes transformative worship may not be what someone else thinks is so. Some may think the ideas in this book are too out-there, beyond their comfort level and too radical a shift away from the status quo. Others may be disappointed I don't go far enough to change everything. What I like is subjective (and worship is a subjective experience). My response to one particular form of worship may relate to my age, ethnic background, or cultural environment, or it may just speak to me. What I like might not necessarily be what others in my generation like and so forth. Still, even with our uniqueness for individual preferences, we can make some generalizations about the religious needs of each generation. I write this book for pastors and leaders of mainline churches who are willing to experiment with alternative forms of worship because they believe God wants their church to reach out and meet the religious needs of another generation of seekers and Christians.

In this introduction, I also offer the following disclaimer: I intend no disrespect to the thousands of current mainline members who think their worship is the way it should be or perceive that worship is not meant to

---

22. I will explore how worship can facilitate this process: creating a setting in which the objective is to develop empathy and ethnic sensitivity through the experiences of others.

Introduction

change people's lives. ("Isn't worship supposed to be boring?") I do not wish to offend anyone by implying these new trends are a "better" or a more "right" way to worship God. I do think we should prayerfully consider alternative forms of worship to convert seekers and enhance the formation of the faith of Christians. Those who want to try some of these suggestions may need to let go of the way they have always done things and manage their anxiety while wandering around in the wilderness (even if a bit aimlessly). By writing this book, I hope to open a window and encourage others to take a look beyond the conventional format and current forms of worship and stretch their imagination to envision new possibilities.

Can we squeeze these new trends into old formats, old buildings, and old people? Is denominational energy better spent on new church ministries given the amount of resistance encountered when leaders introduce change? Isn't it easier to start a new church with new formats, new buildings, and new people than to encourage the faithful members to sacrifice some of their own religious needs so that the needs of others may also be met?[23] Yes it is easier, but I do not believe it is what God is calling us to do. The faithful members of our mainline churches should also be given the opportunity to become disciples and change their lives. I believe they deserve to be part of the process. They are a great resource for the emerging church and should not be left behind in the dust as we plow forward. Most of our current members care deeply about the future of organized religion. They feel frustrated because they don't know what to do to turn the decline around and help their congregation to grow again.

Not everything has to change. A few things about the way we worship *must* change (OK, more than just "a few things"). I will make every attempt to preserve our beloved traditions and rituals as long as the reader is willing to meet me halfway and experiment with new forms of worship. To do this, members have to be willing to change themselves (e.g., become more flexible, open to change, adaptive to new experiences), so that we can change the way we worship to be more conducive to bringing about transformation within the individual.[24] In this model of change, those who have loved and

---

23. It is extremely difficult to change the culture of an organization, especially given the long history of the church. New church starts have the advantage of creating their own culture to be functional from the beginning. For those prayerfully discerning starting a new church, I recommend, *From Zero to One* by Peter Thiel.

24. This is a cyclical process: leaders provide an opportunity to make a change in the individual, and individuals come together to make changes to the organization to be more conducive to changing the individual and are changed in the process.

supported and prayed for the mainline church will also benefit. We will not be casting them aside in favor of the "new people" who have not yet set foot within the church. I hope and pray that mainline members will feel the Holy Spirit moving in their midst so that they will rise up and dance.

This process is not for those looking for an easy, quick, and painless path toward church growth; this process is for those who feel deeply committed to moving the stone away from the tomb. I am not offering gimmicky grabbers to entice people to come to worship.[25] I am also not talking about making changes just for the sake of change (anything is better than this) or to make angry those who insist everyone should want to worship the way they do. Leaders should observe and measure that the changes implemented produce the desired outcome. Not every change effort will work in every context, though most of the ideas in this book cross geographic areas and theological divides. When they don't, I encourage the reader to tweak them to work in your own setting and culture (and then you can write your own book).

What New Trends Are Emerging in Worship?

One of the most significant new trends emerging in worship is an emphasis on designing worship that creates space for a religious *experience*.[26] To allow space for this to occur, transformative worship focuses on the function of worship; that is, what worship is intended to do and how the individual will change as a result of the experience. Particular forms of worship are then explored, sorted through, and selected for their potential to fulfill this function.[27] For example, transformative worship asks: How does praying with our eyes closed and head down help us to hear what God might be saying to us? What is the purpose of prayer? Is it to tell God everything

---

25. In the 1980s and '90s, many congregations took the quick fix approach by investing in praise bands and PowerPoint technology. I am not talking about "contemporary" forms of worship, which will come and go as the tide ebbs and flows, only to appeal to whatever generation is currently moving away from the church. I will not be offering temporary tactics that will magically make all our organizational problems go away. I will be looking at a process by which worship forms will continually be in flux. Even though I cannot be certain that every idea will be generalizable or universal, I will identify religious needs that yearn for expression.

26. See Sweet, *The Gospel According to Starbucks*.

27. One form is often selected over another for no other reasons than "we have always done it this way."

Introduction

that is wrong with our lives and the world so that God will fix it? Is it to make a change within us to be an active participant in God's solution to the problem? Worship leaders can then discern which forms of prayer best assist worshippers to better hear God speaking to them.

Transformative worship seeks to produce a change in the worshippers themselves: moving them along in their spiritual journey, challenging them to see themselves and their situations from a different perspective, and motivating them to carry out acts of social justice. The difference between going to see a counselor and transformative worship (both seek to help people to improve the way they relate to others) is that transformative worship uses theological reflection to make these changes, whereas counseling uses psychology.[28] Undergirding all transformative worship is the mission to equip worshippers to become theologians, capable of thinking theologically about God and the world. While individuals may feel better about themselves by increasing self-esteem, doing theology helps them to discover who they are in relation to Jesus and identify their purpose for being placed on this earth.

Recently, some churches have hired resident theologians, seminary-trained with an extra emphasis on theology, to serve with the leadership of the church (i.e., the pastor). I'm not sure why any church would not see their pastor as the resident theologian, especially one who has graduated from seminary and thus taken courses in theology. Pastors function as resident theologians by doing theology for the worshippers, shaping theological questions and supplying traditional answers. What I see happening in emerging churches is that the pastor is now viewed as the theology professor, teaching the worshippers how to think theologically, how to make sense of ourselves and our interaction with the world around us. Worshippers are becoming resident theologians who share their stories and witness to their experiences of God and invite others to do likewise. Worship provides a learning environment for "how to do theology." Pastors train worshippers by helping them to connect their spiritual experiences with biblical interpretations and historical creeds.

Transformative worship doesn't require a pastor or worship leader to prepare a well-thought-out sermon with all the answers delivered in a neat and concise package. Instead, the pastor explains how he or she arrives at his or her answers and acknowledges there are multiple answers to the same theological question. Pastors also share their personal stories

---

28. Granted both modalities may use theology and psychology, but worship uses more theology than psychology.

(spiritual experiences) and witness to where God is involved and then demonstrate how the Bible provides structure and context to make sense of those experiences. In 1955, people came to church to learn about the Bible to increase their awareness of God's involvement in the world, but today, the trend is reversed: people bring their experiences of God and look toward the church to help them make meaning. As disciples, worshippers feel confident to teach others (spiritual seekers) what they have learned in worship, converting them to Christianity by everything they do both inside and outside of the church.

Transformative worship shifts the responsibility for faith formation from the pastor to the worshipper. Pastors are no longer evaluated for their job performance because they are not to be held accountable for meeting the religious needs of those sitting in the pews.[29] The assessment tool does not ask worshippers, "Did the sermon make you feel better?" or "Did the music put you in a happier mood?" but rather, "What did worship do to challenge your thinking on a particular subject?" and "Do you feel inspired (out of anger, frustration, or guilt/shame) to go out into the community to advocate for the rights of the marginalized and oppressed?" Transformative worship strives to energize people for social justice and community peace-building beyond the objective to make people feel good.[30] Transformative worship is *not* intended to suppress or alleviate difficult feelings but to help people manage them better and direct them as energy to work toward a more equitable society.

Transformative worship does not revolve around a pastor or a worship leader; the focus is not on the chancel but on the worshippers. Pastors do not pour energy into planning every detail of a worship service; instead, they reinvest energy into identifying the gifts, talents, and passions of individual worshippers to serve as leaders at various times throughout the liturgical year. The pastor is the maestro whose movement sets the tempo for each member of the orchestra to play their instruments with passion and pizzazz.[31] While

---

29. What we really need to evaluate is whether these annual evaluations inspire pastors to develop new skill-sets and invoke new energy to implement new ministries, or (as I suspect) they raise the pastor's anxiety that members will criticize their ministry and complain about unstated expectations. Do pastoral evaluations increase (or decrease) the energy between pastor and congregation?

30. My Old Testament professor, William Holliday, used to say, "Is worship really supposed to be a happy party?"

31. One of my favorite books we use for leadership training is *Maestro* by Roger Nierenberg.

INTRODUCTION

the maestro may play the violin with more precision than the first violist, it is not the maestro's function to play each instrument. Instead of doing all the ministry, pastors equip worshippers to lead worship and talk about their faith through witnessing. The function of a pastor/maestro is to inspire all the instrumentalists to hear what others are playing and respond accordingly (rather than focusing solely on their own playing/gifts).

Transformative worship generates energy through interpersonal interaction between worship leaders and worshippers, among worshippers, and between worshippers virtually present and those in cyberspace.[32] What worshippers put into transformative worship is what they get out of it.[33] They are expected to generate as well as respond to this energy (rather than absorb it like sponges). The math can be calculated with the following formula: $1+1=3$ (three times the energy).[34] That energy should be used to go out into the neighborhood to make disciples. We want people to want to be in worship, not to "do their time" so that they can go home and not think about their faith until they have to come back next week.[35] When people complain, "I don't feel spiritually fed by attending worship," I respond, "You can lead a horse to water . . . " We want people to feed each other and not be dependent upon a pastor for the formation of their faith.

Transformative worship tears down the imaginary walls between those who believe in Jesus and those who are unsure what church is all about and where they fit in.[36] It is a style of worship designed for those

32. Transformative worship blurs the lines between the worship leaders and the worshippers. All participants are worshippers but some are designated to lead the direction of the energy.

33. I fear that for too long worshippers have attempted to invest energy into the worship service but because it is not designed for this interaction, it didn't come back to them, so they eventually stopped investing in it.

34. More traditional worship can be calculated as $1-1=0$. The pastor gives one, the worshipper takes one. At the end of the worship service, everyone is tired and wants to go home and take a nap.

35. The problem of inactivity is a result of what is happening in the worship service. The less active they are in worship, the less active they are in participating in other aspects of congregational life and community advocacy and action. Our expectations of what it means to be a Christian have been regular attendance in worship, pledging money, and not constantly criticizing the leadership (and note the similarities with a private country club). Those who become inactive are reporting that worship is boring (and we should check out what they mean by this), irrelevant, and uninspiring. The fastest demographic becoming inactive is no longer our adult children who were raised in the church but active church members who move to a retirement area and do not rejoin a church.

36. Churches that shift to transformative worship will no longer use "the membership

who are looking to have a conversation experience with those who will not judge or tell them that what they believe is right or wrong.[37] This style projects an open atmosphere where we are all travelers on a pilgrimage to encounter God and to make sense of our experiences in order to live spiritually healthy lives. Worshippers find it easy to invite friends and family because those with whom they interact are respectful of others and where they are on this journey. Transformative worship is a public ceremony, a community gathering, and an invitational event for everyone who wants to come and see.

Transformative worship does not assume that every worshipper believes in God or Jesus or accepts every creedal statement of the Christian faith (or has given much thought to what they believe). One does not need to believe in God to attend this style of worship, but all participants are expected to share what they believe and how their experiences shape those beliefs. Gathering for conversation and learning is not geared toward persuasion but listening to the experiences of others. By doing so, we gain insight into our own experiences.[38] Transformative worship doesn't try to convince anyone of anything. Instead, it is a way of worshipping that helps people to sort through the options and figure out what makes sense to them. Transformative worship is a way of worshipping that equips individuals to discern what they believe, surrounded by a great cloud of witnesses.

---

model." They will also move away from membership classes intended to indoctrinate new people "to think the way we think" and preserve the status quo.

37. They can agree or disagree.

38. So much conversation in our culture is to convert others to think the way we do. One of the reasons why some people do not talk about their faith openly is because they have had an experience when someone tried to persuade them to think differently.

Chapter 1

Three Cultural Shifts

Why do we have to change the way we worship?
What has changed in our culture?

FOR THE BUILDER/SILENT GENERATION, the world has changed so dramatically and rapidly over the last fifty years, they are just trying to keep up.[1] What seems like only a short time ago, one had to be sitting in front of a television set to watch a program at the time it was broadcast. Telephones were attached to a squiggly cord plugged into a kitchen wall. The idea that we could shop, do research, play games, and FaceTime with people in faraway lands by surfing a world wide web was inconceivable. Before texting and tweeting, the world felt simpler (and thus more manageable) to this generation. Christians went to church on Sunday morning and spent time with their extended family on Sunday afternoon. Some members want their church to be a refuge from all the changes taking place in society so they invest energy into keeping everything the same. If we could go back to the future in a DeLorean and return to good ol' 1955, most churches would be ready for our arrival.[2]

Every congregation has to discern if they should go-with-the-flow and embrace cultural changes (accommodate) or offer something

---

1. I have loosely divided the generations into three: builder/silent, boomers/Gen X, and millennials. This allows me to identify some of the diversity of religious needs among these three groups.

2. The movie *Back to the Future* was my inspiration for choosing 1955 as a point of reference. It is also within the middle of the time frame members refer to as "the glory days."

counter-cultural (resistance).[3] Do we ask worshippers to turn off their phones or do we find religious uses for them? Do we write new rap or alternative punk music to reflect Christian themes or do we insist everyone sing hymns in the "Rock of Ages" genre? Do we make worship ultra-familiar for millennials and risk making it ultra-foreign for the builder/silent generation? Are spiritual seekers looking for something they can relate to or something new and different? I suggest churches upgrade their technology so that it enhances the worship experience (there's nothing worse than bad technology in worship) and offer opportunities to engage others in the virtual world. Transformative worship balances using technology with creating space for personal, meaningful interactions between worshippers. In an age when we are dependent upon technology as a means of connection with others, the church can provide a unique experience (i.e., non-technological interaction).

Some insist that the mission before us is to convince millennials to want to worship as if it is still 1955. These congregations focus their efforts on changing spiritual seekers: if only they would show up at the front door on Sunday morning, members could relive the glory days. Other congregations are realizing that in order to turn around the decline, they will need to be the ones willing to change. The current members are challenged with the work of sorting through the rummage sale and deciding what to keep, what to recycle or repurpose, what has a shelf-life and what needs to be trashed, so that the church can lighten its load to move forward.[4] The problem is that in our anxiety over the decline, we have become a bunch of hoarders, clinging to outdated traditions held to be sacrosanct. As a result, congregations are experiencing a heightened sense of resistance to change, and when leaders attempt to make changes to attract spiritual seekers, they are likely to encounter sabotage and conflict. We need to be clear about why changes should be made and who stands to benefit.

Why Do We Have to Change the Way We Worship?

It matters why we want to make changes to the way we worship. No one wants to worship with pouting members trying to tolerate contemporary music because they were told by their pastor that this is the only way to save the church. No one wants to worship with grouchy people more concerned

---

3. For the most part, mainline churches have accommodated to cultural changes.
4. See Tickle, *The Great Emergence*.

with the maintenance of an organization than exploring new ways to experience God. I have come to appreciate how the worshippers' attitudes and emotions contribute to the worship experience. Visitors can sense how worshippers feel about their church. They observe how worshippers interact with one another and with the pastor and how much effort is expended to develop relationships with new people. Transformative worship is not an exercise in doing the minimum effort to produce the maximum benefit (e.g., offering praise music to attract more members); it is an effort to discern new ways to experience God which will form, renew, and reform the faith of all participants.

Many congregations are making changes to the way they worship with the hope of attracting young families. This puts too much pressure on the millennials to be the messianic generation who will compensate for their parents' generation who never went to church (Gen X) or their grandparents who became frustrated and left (boomers). Current members from the builder/silent generations try to guess what the millennials are looking for and end up frustrated because their efforts are not attracting them to worship. When the millennials don't show up on cue, members may even blame them for the decline. Still worse, I hear statements such as "young families today don't make church a priority," and "they don't make commitments like we do."[5] Thinking that the missing generation is responsible for their predicament (and their anxiety) only reinforces the fear among seekers that those who attend church are judgmental and hypercritical. Our starting point is to confront our own misperceptions.

The denial is thick and fears about the future run deep. Uncertainty about what lies ahead hangs heavy over the sanctuary.[6] Mainline decline is seen as a problem to be solved by increasing worship attendance and an obstacle to be overcome by motivating people to give more money to the church. In the meantime, members suggest making their pastor part time to save money (just in case things get worse before they get better). The

---

5. The millennials are just as commitment-oriented as other generations. It is a falsehood that the generations following the builder/silent are not as loyal to the things they care about. These generations are just as deeply committed as their parents and grandparents; they care about different things. For instance, millennials are more relationally committed to significant others than they are to organizations. They look for opportunities to have healthy interactions with their family and friends. Any organization that can offer these relational opportunities as its mission is likely to engage them.

6. Numerically growing a congregation is not as difficult as is often perceived. What is difficult is changing the mind-set of members to act like disciples.

decline in membership, finances, and resources is driving an intense need to hold tight to "the way we have always done things" and regress to a former glory (remembered as a less anxious time). To turn things around, we need to view mainline decline as a sign that what we are offering is not what people are looking for from a religious organization. If what we are growing is not producing fruit, we need new seeds and a new way to harvest them. We need to be open to doing things differently and trust that the Holy Spirit is moving us along to discover new ways of being the church.

What Has Changed?

There are three significant cultural shifts impacting the way we worship God in Jesus Christ. They are as follows and I will address each of them in this chapter.

1. A shift from a culture of obligation to a culture of choice. Once people were given a choice, religious organizations have to offer something people need.
2. A shift in the way people relate to organizations. They no longer form their identity through membership but bring "who they are" (identity) into the organization.
3. A shift from paper and electronics to technology.

The Shift from a Culture of Obligation to a Culture of Choice

I remember the day I decided to assert my independence and test out the limits of teenage rebellion. "I am *not* going to church. It's boring and I don't want to go." My mother, looking traumatized by such an act of defiance, responded "Laurene Beth, you go upstairs and get dressed this minute. You *are* going to church." I stomped up the stairs expressing my opposition. There were times when I went to church because I felt someone was twisting my arm (and I still felt that way as a pastor!), because as long as there was a cultural norm embedded in our society that said "you *have* to go to church," everyone went somewhere. The processional of kicking and screaming teenagers being dragged into church by parents who really didn't want to be there either is not our finest scenario for evangelism. I realize some people enjoy going to church and feel they receive something of substance by attending worship. But in a culture of obligation, it didn't matter if worship met one's religious needs because "you had to go anyway."

Most of our current membership continues to attend worship out of a sense of obligation. They have been attending since they were children. Members of their extended family also attend this church and have done so for several generations. They express their sentiment toward the congregation with the same devotion as they feel toward their family. Gather a group of leaders from a mainline church and ask them, "How did you come to this church?" They will talk about their family histories, with ancestral roots reaching deep and wide. They will recall what the church has meant to their families, memories of previous pastors, and the interpersonal relationships they cherish with other members. Members identify why they attend worship in terms of relationships with other members, especially those who have been a source of emotional support during times of tragedy and tribulation. They have no experience of waking up one day and feeling something spiritual is missing from their lives and wondering if the church has something to offer them to fill this void.

This makes it more difficult for members to figure out what would inspire someone to choose to attend a worship service. They assume new members will come in the same way in which they came (e.g., through birth, moving to a new neighborhood, or transferring membership from one denominationally affiliated church to another). This thinking enables the "wait until they show up" and "build it and they will come" attitudes toward evangelism. Today, however, very few people are showing up at the front door on their own volition. They no longer feel the societal tug that says, "One should go to church on Sunday morning," and they can think of a thousand other activities they could be doing (e.g., catching up on needed sleep, running errands, or watching television and relaxing). In current economic circumstances, many people work more than one full time job.

In a culture of obligation, worship attendance was an expectation of membership (as was pledging to the annual budget). Few asked why we worship the way we do or thought about exploring options or experimenting with new forms. There was no urgency to assess whether the forms of worship were meeting the religious needs of the current membership, never mind the community at large. To be concerned with what the church has to offer to its neighborhood would have seemed irrelevant (and challenging the way the pastor led worship might have seemed irreverent). To wonder what seekers are looking for was not likely a topic of conversation at the consistory meeting. In these days, there were very few people who did not attend a religious organization. To research and identify motivational factors for why members and seekers attend church (and some factors are the same, some different) is one of the most important tasks for revitalization in a culture of choice.

When neighbors inquire, "Why do you go to the First Baptist Church?" members often say, "Because I have a lot of friends there."[7] Neighbors are likely to respond to an invitation by saying, "I don't need to go to your church. I already have enough friends." (If all we have to offer is friendship, we are in trouble!). Millennials make friends on the internet, at the cafes and bars, while attending college or employed by a large corporation. Whereas the builder/silent generation moved into a neighborhood and then attended church to meet their neighbors, the younger generations have several other avenues for social interaction (which do not involve joining an organization). My parents would often say "the church is the center of our social life" but my generation would not think of the church as a place to meet people. If what the church has to offer to millennials is friendship and that's not what they are looking for, we have found one of the gaps.

I encourage members to refrain from using friendship language to refer to their communion with one another as a congregation. While these relationships are important, they really are not "friends." They have formed stronger ties binding them as a faith community who prays together and is intentional about allowing the Holy Spirit to work through them. For this reason, some churches refer to these relationships as "sisters and brothers in Christ" to emphasize the religious connectedness from shared beliefs. We need to find ways to support worshippers in relating to each other on a more personal level, which involves intimate sharing and active listening to improve their capacity for empathy. Not everyone relates to their friends by being open and honest. As sisters and brothers in Christ, we do not need to hide our struggles or put on a brave face, but can be ourselves with all our weakness and still be loved and accepted.

To numerically grow a congregation, the pastor and leaders should equip members to be able to clearly articulate the answer to the question, "How do these relationships contribute to faith formation?" In a culture of choice, framing what worship is intended to do is the way we advertise our

---

7. Once the culture shifted to choice, members began looking for reasons to explain their behavior of weekly worship attendance in ways that were new to them because they didn't have to do this in a culture of obligation.

product. The most significant difference between congregations that are growing and those in decline is that leaders know their mission field, have prayed about how to reach out to them, and are well aware of what they are looking for from the church. Instead of being concerned with "helping them to get to know us," the focus is on "helping us get to know them" (and showing interest and concern for the community). Membership classes are replaced by discipleship training, which shifts the focus away from acclimating new people to fit into organizational structures to forums that help disciples to identify the religious needs of seekers.

The Shift Away from Membership

If we were to go with Marty and Doc back to 1955, we would find a very different culture than the one we live in today. While people exercise the same strength of commitment to the things they care about, the amount of time we are willing to commit ourselves is less than in 1955.[8] Whereas the builder/silent generation worked for the same company most of their lives, today people work for one company for a few years and then move on to another. Years ago, pastors graduated from seminary, received a call to a particular congregation, and when they died were buried in the cemetery in the church's backyard. Today, pastors move from one church to another with a fluidity reflecting this cultural shift away from long-term commitments. This shift is evidenced throughout our culture. When the builder/silent generation purchased a home, they paid off a thirty-year mortgage and lived in their house for as long as they were able to care for themselves. Younger generations buy and sell property as they move from one job to the next.

The builder/silent generation joined organizations such as churches, synagogues, or temples to practice their religious beliefs but they also joined civic organizations, bowling leagues, and scouting (which was also a way to express patriotism). They played sports, voted in elections, and attended parent/teacher associations and events (and frequently volunteered to support these organizations). If they were Protestant men, they were Masons. Then in 1964, everything changed. Robert Putman in *Bowling Alone* shows how individuals were increasingly involved with these organizations until 1964, and then participation curves downward as membership decreases (a trend

---

8. Few today want to commit to serving on a committee for three years.

which continues to this day).[9] Putman correlates this finding with the fact that in 1964 almost every American household owned a television set and now could stay home to watch programs as a way to connect with the outside world. The television gave people their first option not to attend church.

The way people relate to organizations has also changed. Prior to 1964, people joined social, civil, and religious organizations as "members" to participate in the life of the community and to feel they were making a difference (which gave them a sense of belonging). Selecting a particular organization to become a member of is still important to the formation of identity for the builder/silent generation. In other words, "who I am" and "who I am in relation to God and others" is defined by which organizations they participate and invest energy, money, and time. Those who are now transitioning to heaven (who die in their seventies or older) summarize their lives in an obituary by listing their organizational affiliations. "She was a member of the Presbyterian Church." "He was an Eagle Scout." "He served in the Navy during World War II." The builder/silent generation formed their identity through the organizations to which they belonged.

The boomer/Gen X generation does not share their parents' and grandparents' interest in joining social, civic, or religious organizations. They tend to form identity through their vocation (and were more likely to have the opportunity to attend college and choose a vocation than the builder/silent generation). They join professional organizations that can help them advance their career and offer support (e.g., academic journals and continuing education). Organizational affiliations are often obligatory in order to improve one's vocational skills and schmooze with the right people who can help one get a promotion. Several vocations require these memberships (e.g., National Association of Social Workers) to purchase malpractice insurance or grant authorization to practice a skill. A member may know another member from a conference but most members have never met face-to-face.

Millennials don't form their identity through organizations *or* through their vocation (or the organizations which support that vocation). They are more likely to form their identity through significant relationships. An organization is merely a forum for developing and interacting with other people in the formation of their identity. They resist organizations that generate a "groupthink" rather than encourage independent thinking. They have little interest in organizations that insist everyone has to agree (especially with

---

9. See Putnam, *Bowling Alone*.

Three Cultural Shifts

those who are in authority) and look for places which inspire creative and innovative thinking with a critical eye toward outdated thinking (e.g., prejudice toward one group, global warming is a myth, etc.). They believe in God and don't see what difference it would make to attend a religious organization to be told to believe in God. They are suspicious of religious organizations that "tell people what to believe" in an effort to get everyone to think the same way.

Millennials are also unaware of how to go about joining organizations and often assume that one has to be invited to attend or at least sponsored by another member.[10] It would not occur to them to show up on Sunday morning as an unexpected (or unwanted) guest. To do so would be like showing up for a party that one was not invited to attend. You just wouldn't do it (and we wonder why they are not showing up for worship). They don't know anyone who attends a religious organization (other than their grandmother) and consider it unlikely that someone their age would invite them. In a culture that says, "You don't walk on someone else's property without their permission," they would not trespass onto church property without an invitation. They have followed their parents' legacy of not being joiners but may show interest in an organization that uses a different model of belonging than membership.

The organizational structure of the emerging church is not based on hierarchy with a senior-something down to a youth group leader. They do not collect dues/pledges and there is no membership roll. Counting how many people show up for worship is no longer an indicator of congregational health; rather, leaders carefully monitor momentum and encourage members to become disciples by inviting others because they are excited about new forms of worship. The emerging church is not tied to a building nor does it use most of its income to heat the building, refurbish the organ, or repair the steeple. The emerging church will not be connected to a wider body which makes decisions to pass down to the members, informing them how to think and what to do. Denominational structures are becoming irrelevant and in time, will be obsolete. Some churches will continue to be in covenant if to do so is mutually beneficial to reaching their mission field.

Many of the conventional forms with which we worship reflect denominational affiliation. The historical background for this was so that a member could attend a worship service in another church of the same

---

10. Meanwhile, the builder/silent generation says, "They don't need an invitation. They should just come."

denomination and follow the liturgy because it was the same as in their home church.[11] One knew what to expect from the service and what was expected as a worshipper (e.g., everyone knows that an asterisk in a bulletin means one should stand, if able). Pastors were expected to preach on the same scriptural passages from the lectionary as a way to connect with the wider church.[12] This practice remains prevalent today and most denominations continue to provide written liturgy for their pastors and worship leaders to use so that every church is on the same page.[13] I sincerely doubt this practice will continue in the emerging church, although we need new forms of teaching and preaching (which could be provided by the denomination) to improve biblical literacy among Christians.

Most denominations have also invested money and energy into what is known as "branding" in order to differentiate themselves from other denominations. If the problem-to-be-solved is that spiritual seekers don't know which denomination to join, then branding would be an effective solution. If those of the millennial generation, which tends to be drawn to liberal, progressive churches because of their position on marriage equality, inadvertently found themselves in a conservative or fundamentalist worship service, then branding would assist them on their search for a different kind of church (but these categories are becoming less relevant).[14] Branding may raise "a bold voice" for social justice but there is no evidence that the millennial generation cares what the church thinks on these matters.[15] A bigger problem for the denominations that are paying for branding to attract millennials to their churches is that they are asking, "What's a denomination?"

In 1955, denominational branding, through trademark symbols, taglines, and commercials of inclusivity made sense when the culture began to shift so that individuals had a choice beyond the denomination of their parents' affiliation. As a nation, we were divided into Protestant, Catholic, and Jewish. For most of our history, we have been a predominantly Christian nation. Protestants, the numerically largest subgroup, further divided into Congregational or Episcopalian or Methodist, etc. But as our nation becomes

---

11. The liturgy is a historical imprint expressing a denomination's uniqueness.

12. The lectionary covers about 60 percent of the Bible and is on a three-year cycle. .

13. Members knew the same hymns, service format, liturgical procession, and preaching style because the worship leaders graduated from the same seminary.

14. See Putman and Campbell, *American Grace*.

15. For a while, the conservative voice predominated and young people assumed it was reflective of all Christians.

more pluralistic today, shifting demographics to embody a significant increase in Buddhists, Hindus, Muslims, and Wiccans, people are now identifying themselves by their religion and, if Protestant, not by their denomination. To confirm what I am talking about, note how millennials refer to their religious identity on Facebook (e.g., "Christian"). Using denomination as a point of religious distinction is therefore becoming extraneous.[16]

Millennials are less interested in limiting their religiosity to one particular religion at the expense of learning about the spiritual practices of other global religions. They are curious to try spiritual meditation from Buddhism and wonder what puja is like for Hindu culture (a sacred ritual of worship in one's home). They resist the idea that they have to choose one religious practice over others, especially if they find new ways of encountering God. They search for innovative ways to express their faith on the internet or practice yoga at the local health club. Unlike the generations before them who feared that the roof would cave in if they attended a worship service in a church of a different faith, millennials feel the freedom to explore and experiment with different religious practices. Transformative worship inspires curiosity and respect for what others believe. Seekers can then make an informed decision about which religion makes sense for them.

The Shift from Electronic to Technology

My father, who represents the builder/silent generation, recalls the days when his family gathered around the living room, in the shadow of a roaring fire from the hearth to listen to a program, a sitcom or news broadcast on the radio. His generation did this for hours, listening to the comedy of Lucille Ball and Milton Berle, hearing news from around the world, and a play-by-play of a baseball game. "It was like it was happening right in my own living room," he would say. The idea that a small box could receive transmitted signals of sound across many miles was the model of high-tech sophistication and brought a heightened sense of connectedness with others. As a result, the builder/silent generation developed the auditory skill to hear words and attach them to mental representations in order to make sense of what is being said. They could imagine a scene as another was describing it.

---

16. In the churches I served in Massachusetts, there were people who attended worship faithfully and considered themselves "practicing Catholics." Even the difference between being Protestant and Catholic is fading away.

So when the builder/silent generation comes to church to sit in a pew (like sitting in a living room but less comfortable) they possess the auditory skill to listen to a sermon preached from the pulpit. Because they could listen to a program on the radio for thirty or sixty minute segments, they could listen for thirty minutes to a sermon and sixty minutes to a worship service. Whatever the pastor was talking about (e.g., Jesus walking on the water or feeding the five thousand), this generation could envision the scene and didn't need a PowerPoint to do it for them. (They tend to resent images being superimposed as if their own image is less valid.) The builder/silent generation listens throughout a worship service, can form a mental representation of what is being said and thinks about what they are saying in the responsive liturgy. They do not understand why the younger generations cannot do likewise.

The boomer/Gen X generation grew up watching television. From the Monkees to the Partridge Family, Saturday Night Live to Full House, we relax by sitting back on our sofa and turning on the tube. My generation listens to some talk radio but only if we are in the car (on Sirius); otherwise we listen to music. We fast forward over commercials and almost never watch a television show at the time it airs (preferring to DVR). If the television breaks, as long as it's not the picture tube, we could still watch (without the sound). On the treadmill at the gym, I can watch television (which I do almost every morning) while listening to music on my iPod. I can surmise what is going on (even watching the news) because television stations know that my generation is not necessarily listening to the program. Captions are provided at the bottom of the screen so that we do not easily lose interest and surf for another channel. Most of my television watching is done with the mute button on while I am doing something else (e.g., reading or shopping online).

Boomers/Gen X did not develop the same auditory skills as the builder/silent generation. We cannot hear something and imagine what is being said. When the pastor is talking about Jesus walking on the water, we are not picturing the scene in our minds because our imagination doesn't work that way. When we read the congregation's response to a liturgy printed in bold letters, we are not consciously thinking about what we are saying (just as when we sing the lyrics of any rock or pop song). We are repeating the words out loud, but they don't mean anything to us because we are not actively converting them to comprehension. We come to church and have little interest in listening to a twenty-minute sermon much less sitting

THREE CULTURAL SHIFTS

through an entire sixty-minute worship service. Our minds drift . . . and as a result, we are drifting away from organized religion.

The two technical fixes of the contemporary worship movement, a praise band and a PowerPoint projector, were valiant attempts to keep members in their forties, fifties, and sixties interested in coming to church (even if the initial intention was to attract the millennials to worship).[17] Churches purchased big screens and hung them so that they could be released from the chancel (much to the disgust of the builder/silent generation). As the liturgist reads the scripture of Jesus calling the children into his midst and the visual pops up on the screen showing a picture or a YouTube clip, the boomer/Gen X generation connects what is being said with a visual representation. We think to ourselves, "Oh, now I get it." While these technical fixes might keep some from our generation attending church, neither had much success in attracting spiritual seekers of any generation.

The boomer/Gen X generation loves to see sanctuaries decorated with creative, brightly colored banners, quilts with images of Jesus carrying the lost sheep back to the flock, tulle strung in a twisted pattern from the front of the chancel to the back of the church, etc. All forms of art, painting, pottery, and sculpture, preferably being created during the worship service, captivate our imagination and invoke our spiritual wonderings. Even better is when worship participants have the opportunity to create their own painting/art piece of how they visualize Jesus praying in the garden or walking on the road to Emmaus. We watch HGTV and like natural light streaming through the big windows as well as updated kitchens and restrooms. My generation subscribes to the Marcia McPhee Worship Design Studio.[18] Her ideas inspire worship leaders to be creative and imaginative to produce a multisensory experience of worship.

Whereas the builder/silent generation listened to world events broadcasted from a nearby radio station and the boomer/Gen X generation watches television, the millennials are living in a very different technological environment. They do not only listen and watch: they interact with technology. They like to vote for their favorite American idol and they contribute information to Wikipedia. Emailing is falling out of vogue and texting is being replaced with voice commands. All the old public phone booths are being torn down in New York City to construct links so that

---

17. In other words, the boomer/Gen X generation projected what they thought the millennials would be attracted to, when they were talking about their own religious needs.

18. See http://www.worshipdesignstudio.com.

everyone walking down the street has access to the world wide web. The level at which individuals can interact with one another has changed so dramatically that the idea of sitting in a pew in an old building without any internet access and being asked to turn off one's phone seems so passé.

Millennials stay current with technology and expect up-to-date modes of communication from any organization or business. Low-tech attempts to be "cool" turn them away and high-tech attempts to attract them may feel contrived. Technology should be used in the worship service to facilitate understanding and knowledge but not as a substitute for face-to-face (physical and not just virtual) interaction. This is not an either-or issue: either we accommodate by installing technology or resist by insisting people turn off their devices. We need to offer both. Where technology overruns the worship experience, millennials wonder why they need to come to church (e.g., "I can watch YouTube videos at home."). Face-to-face personal encounters without technology are less available in our society. Therefore, the church should use technology but also offer opportunities for interpersonal interaction.

These three cultural shifts are having a huge impact on the way we do church, especially when we take into consideration the experiences of these three generations and the skill sets they have developed as a result of advances in technology. Every congregation needs to be flexible so that they can make changes that will appeal across the generations of all believers and seekers. The challenge before us is to generate a willingness to try new things, take risks, and model for those in the community how faith formation changes peoples' lives. Members become disciples when they are willing to change themselves in order to be change agents in the community. In this light, the body of Christ functions as a fluid organism continually readapting to its surround in order to remain relevant for each generation's religious needs.

Chapter 2

The Church's Mission

Why does the church exist?
What does it mean to be a Christian today?
What difference does being a Christian make in one's life?
What does the church have to offer to those who are seeking?

IN 1955, THE CHURCH had a purpose but obligation drove attendance and participation. Once culture provided an option of choice, an organization's mission has to be well-articulated to attract new people. Every member should be clear about why the church exists.[1] Then they know what the church has to offer to spiritual seekers in order to change their lives. They do this by talking about how the church has changed their lives. For instance, a disciple may invite a seeker by saying,

> I too was going through a really difficult time in my life when I felt overwhelmed by all the crises happening one after another. It felt like I landed face down on the ground, and someone from the church invited me to a worship service where they offer spiritual support groups. I found hope that day because others shared with me how they saw God involved in my story. I feared God had abandoned me or worse, that God was punishing me for something I had done wrong. By studying the Bible, experiencing God through others, and identifying with their stories, I came to a new place of strength and courage. It sounds like you feel as overwhelmed as I

---

1. These congregations bring me in to ask for "quick fix" tactics for church growth and become frustrated when I start talking about the church's mission as our starting point.

did and so I'm wondering if you would like to come with me to a worship service on Sunday.

To begin the conversation about what the church has to offer to the community, I encourage every member to enter into a time of prayer. Some churches have instituted "prayer partners" or "prayer triads." Individuals are linked together so they have someone to pray and talk with about how the answers are revealed through prayer. The congregation should also pray together during worship to discern what they believe God is calling them to do. I use the image of putting together a puzzle. God reveals one puzzle piece to each member through prayer to cast the vision for what the church will look like as it embarks on this new journey. Everyone needs to be engaged in this process to discern God's vision.[2]

When the demographics change in a neighborhood, from one ethnic group to another or toward multiple groups of diversity, some congregations do not seem to notice. Members assume they know who lives in the neighborhood as if it is still 1955. They haven't updated their perceptions to accurately reflect the current demographics. Some members have moved out of the neighborhood. They now expect people from their new neighborhood to commute to the church.[3] They comment that the new demographic of seekers are not "like" them and therefore unlikely to attend the church.[4] So they either wait for the neighborhood to change back or decide there is nothing they can do but close the church. Yet, there is another option: they can try to reach a different mission field than they have reached in the past.

For those congregations that want to know who is living in the neighborhood, I recommend using a demographic report.[5] These reports answer the questions: who is out there and what are they looking for from a church? The company collects data from a variety of sources (e.g., Experian, national census) and then correlates variables to be useful to understand the religious needs of a neighborhood. MissionInsite contains a document written by Tom Bandy (a guru in the field of church growth), which interprets the data to

---

2. The vision is a picture of what the church will look like when the mission is in motion.

3. The reason they are commuting is because they have a relationship with the congregation and the setting. They are unlikely to get others to travel some distance who have no emotional tie to either.

4. According to Pew research, there are more Latino Protestants living in the United States than Episcopalians. I often hear members comment, "All Latinos are Catholic."

5. I use http://www.missioninsite.com.

identify religious needs based on "mosaic groups" used by Experian.[6] His ideas range from how the pastor is expected to exercise leadership, how seekers want to be approached, and even what to serve at coffee hour. The premise is that different generations are looking for different things from a church.[7] There is no "one strategy fits all" approach. The way we reach out for invitational ministry, the style of worship, and how we convert people to Christianity need to be tailored to be effective in each church's cultural environment.

The demographics also provide a theological foundation for the mission: Why does God want this church to continue to serve this neighborhood? If the demographics have changed (e.g., with respect to ethnicity), and this change is not reflected in the current membership, then the congregation has a decision to make whether or not to work passionately to bring in new members who reflect the current demographics. These reports also identify what the community is praying about (e.g., life concerns), and give the congregation a glimpse of what kinds of invitational events to hold in order to address these concerns. MissionInsite also has a section on why those in the community have lost interest in church. All this information is helpful in trying to discern the mission of a particular church in a particular social location. Whomever God has placed in the neighborhood is God's gift to the future of a church.

Some congregations will identify what spiritual seekers in the community are looking for but not feel called to make substantial changes to their worship service to meet those needs. They may also not feel they have enough energy (e.g., "these are great ideas but who is going to do them?"). When everyone in the congregation feels depleted of energy and not hopeful that using more energy is likely to produce the desired result, they continue an inward focus or make the painful (but freeing) decision to let go and close the church. What they should not do is sit back and wait for the new people to arrive at the front door and when they don't show make negative statements about why they are not doing so.[8] The only unfaithful decision is not to decide. So many congregations want to do a turnaround, but what they really want is for new people to come without making any changes to the way they worship. I am talking about making substantial

---

6. http://missioninsite.com/missionimpact-guide/.

7. These reports are also based on geography, ethnicity, economic circumstance, etc.

8. Most congregations wish I would wave a magic wand and they would have a hundred new people in worship on Sunday morning. I have come to realize that this is also their greatest fear.

changes to the culture of the church as an organization. These changes are not for the faint of heart or for those "just trying to keep the doors open."

What Is the Mission of the Church?

Several denominations have adopted the tagline that their purpose is to "change people's lives." This is like saying, "We have something to offer but we are not going to tell you what it is until you show up for worship or you can tell us what you think our purpose might be because we are still trying to figure it out." These days, it is not enough to promote the church as an organization that provides personal transformation without reference to the specific process used to enact this change. Spiritual seekers want to know, "How is the church going to assist me to change my life?" and "What will happen in worship to enhance my faith formation and help me to be more empathic toward the struggles of others?"[9] I often hear, "If God is everywhere, what will the church *do* to help me change my life that I cannot do alone in the sanctity of my backyard?"

There is way too much swirly talk by denominations, reflected in congregations, about changing people's lives and not enough practical, down-to-earth, authentic, concrete, relevant application. In the first five minutes of worship, spiritual seekers want to hear exactly how this service is designed to change their lives. They want to know the direction the worship leaders are leading (or why follow?). Those who have little or no experience attending worship do not know what leaders are implying when they make such bold statements as "we are in the business of changing people's lives" and may fear brainwashing tactics. They already fear that leaders will become aggressive in their attempt at conversion. They wonder, "If I sit through this worship service, how am I going to be a different person in the next hour or is this just a lot of talk to try to convince me to come back next Sunday?"

The mission of the church is a two-step process: to assist spiritual seekers to convert to Christianity and to equip Christians to put their beliefs into practice. Conversion is to a set of core beliefs and is a prerequisite for Christian practice. Therefore, this process is linear from point A (spiritual seeking) to point B (believing in the core beliefs of Christianity) to point C (putting beliefs into Christian practice). Essentially, what one believes

---

9. Good preaching helps worshippers relate to a story and feel that the preacher understands their situation (emotionally). Great preaching equips worshippers to be empathic toward the situations of others.

influences social, moral, and philosophical issues and thus impacts the way in which a Christian behaves and acts in the world (e.g., to promote equality, alleviate poverty, and save the planet from the effects of global warming). What we believe is connected with what we do, and when we do what we do, those beliefs should be articulated as the driving force. Our beliefs are made manifest through our willingness to take risks, make sacrifices for the good of others, and go beyond acts of charity to actions of social justice.

If what we believe has no bearing on what we do, or perhaps worse, if what we believe is incongruent with what we do, then being a Christian doesn't make much difference to ourselves or to the world. Some of my best friends who are social workers are also avowed atheists and among the most compassionate and caring people I know. They claim they do not need a core set of beliefs to tell them how to behave and help other people. They perceive they contribute to the well-being of the universe more than the Christian who goes to church to request forgiveness on Sunday morning and then reenters into the corporate world to play by a different set of ethical rules. Believers of other religions (e.g., Islam, Buddhism, Judaism), have also done great things for humanity, no less and no more than those who adhere to Christianity. So what difference does conversion to Christianity make? If I can't tell a Christian from an atheist or someone who says they are "spiritual but not religious," then is Christianity nothing more than a self-serving set of beliefs that provide me with comfort and assurance that I am loved by God in Christ Jesus or that I hold the holy ticket to get into heaven?

Conversion to Christianity and application of a belief system is geared toward helping Christians to live spiritually healthy lives which inspire them to practice compassion, love, generosity and hospitality. This is not to say that Christians are happier than others, but they feel more satisfied with their lives because they are fully aware of why they do the things they do. Christians should be able to balance self-care with other-concern, constantly monitoring their behavior for indiscretions and inconsistencies. We experience inner-peace through a personal relationship with Jesus Christ and that relationship is the foundation for how we interact with other people. Being a Christian benefits the world and offers a counter-cultural option to the pursuit of narcissism. In a culture of individualism and all that entails, the Christian life promotes a sense of connectedness, which values concern about others in the same light as concern for self.

What Does It Mean to Be a Christian?

If the church's mission is to convert spiritual seekers to Christianity and to apply these beliefs to practice, then we should identify what makes someone a Christian. When I ask a group of members attending a church growth workshop what it means to them to be a Christian today, these are common responses:

"to be compassionate and practice loving kindness";

"to treat other people the way I would want to be treated";

"to do what Jesus would do, to use his teachings as a guidebook for daily living";

"to take care of the poor, marginalized, and oppressed";

"to follow the Ten Commandments and focus on Jesus's greatest commandment to love God, our neighbors, and ourselves."

Interesting to note, these statements represent a set of *behaviors* (some with their corresponding motivational factors). Yet, one does not necessarily have to be Christian to practice being compassionate or taking care of the poor. To be kind toward others is practiced by most people regardless of religious affiliation.[10] This is not to say these behaviors are not important to practicing Christianity, only to observe that many who do not believe in the Christian faith exhibit these same acts and are faithful members of a different religious community.[11] In other words, these behaviors do not set us apart from other belief systems or identify our uniqueness as Christians.[12]

---

10. The so called "Golden Rule" is practiced in almost every global religion. In other words, the ethical conduct of interpersonal interaction, which deems that we should use ourselves as a guide to how to treat others, is a universal presupposition.

11. Ask members to play "identify the Christian." Bring in two people, one who is an atheist and another who is a devout Christian (and this can be a role play). What kinds of questions would you ask to try to figure out who is the atheist and who is the Christian? Or better yet, between a Muslim and a Christian or a Jew and a Christian? What are some of the perimeters that define what it means to be a Christian in distinction from other religions? If someone is a Christian at work, and being a Christian is about manifesting a core set of behaviors, could I tell the difference between the Christian and the atheist?

12. If we could do a research project and show that Christians are spiritually healthier, more social-justice oriented, and kinder and more compassionate than a control group of non-Christians, then it would be relatively easy to convert people to Christianity. If the behavior of Christians is more generous than the behavior of non-Christians, we wouldn't be having this conversation. In fact, those within Christianity have committed some atrocious crimes as of late, blemishing organized religion in its failure to implement

Further, by focusing almost exclusively on behavior we may be subliminally implying that Christian religion functions as a superego to keep us on the straight and narrow. Do we need religion to teach us to be helpful to others? Are we only being compassionate because the Bible tells us to or because we fear the heavenly repercussions for not doing so? Does it matter why we do what we do as Christians? Does being a Christian make a difference in the quality of the help we offer? By reducing religion to a particular set of behaviors, spiritual seekers are saying, "I don't need to come to church. I am already a good person." They perceive that the church tells people how to behave and outlines the differences between right and wrong. If one is already practicing good moral and ethical behavior, what benefit would there be to attending worship and listening to a sermon outlining the rules?

If I were to ask members this same question in 1955, I would have heard different answers. These members (many now among the saints) did not define being a Christian in terms of behaviors (with the exception of attending church and pledging). Instead, they would have focused on a core set of beliefs. The following is a 1955 sample of likely responses to the question, "What makes someone a Christian?"

"to believe in Jesus Christ";

"to believe Jesus is the incarnation of God";

"to believe in the Trinitarian formula of God the Father, Jesus the Son, and the Holy Spirit the Sustainer";

"to believe the Bible is the Word of God";

"to believe that we are all loved equally by God";

"to believe God created the world."

What it meant to be a Christian in 1955 was to accept a core set of beliefs. Members rallied together because they believed in Christian creeds. To further identify themselves, they crafted testimonies to promote denominational distinction (e.g., the United Church of Christ's statement of faith). Christian education programs for children and youth flourished because

---

safe-church policies. We are even seeing more conflict within churches, escalating to the point where the most dysfunctional people are given free-reign to wreak havoc upon the health of the organization. Those within religious organizations are not always better adjusted to life or handle its traumas and crises more adaptively than those who find their spirituality in other places.

forming faith was a priority of what it meant to become a Christian. After a transitional mark of conversion (i.e., confirmation), Christians attended worship, Bible study, and adult Sunday school to enhance biblical literacy because these practices strengthen one's faith. Members also accepted a set of behaviors for ethical conduct, but their beliefs would have informed these behaviors. Jesus' teachings through parables and stories provided them guidance and wisdom for how to reach out and show compassion toward those who are suffering.

This is not to say that current members do not believe in Jesus Christ or his divinity. Since 1955, we have shifted from focusing on *beliefs* to *behaviors*, and consequently, disconnected the two. One of the major reasons mainline is in decline is that there has been too much emphasis on behaviors and too little emphasis on beliefs. This is evident when denominations brand themselves as agents of social justice with no mention of the beliefs that inspire them to choose one side of a sociopolitical debate. Denominational agencies contribute to resolving contemporary global and social problems, a source of pride among their affiliated congregations, but they are virtually silent on *why* they engage in such activity.[13] Whereas faith without works is futile, works without (articulating) faith is not religion. The task before us is to reclaim our identity as a religious organization and reconnect our beliefs with our behaviors.

The connection between beliefs and behaviors is an important one, given the feedback we often hear from spiritual seekers that Christians do not practice what they preach (and certainly none of us could do this all the time!). They see Christians on the outside of the church exhibiting selfish motives and cannot tell the difference between what a Christian does from anyone else. They see Christians holding signs promoting hate, inequality, and violence, and they don't want to be part of any organization which thinks it has the right to judge others (especially when those decisions

---

13. From the perspective of millennials, religion has not played a role in the solutions to societal problems. Worse, they perceive that too often religion drives the escalation of conflict. Who wants to join an organization that has historically pillaged whole communities, led crusades of righteous indignation, wreaked an aura of superiority, and allowed the sexual victimization of children? What makes adherents of religious organizations perceive they rate higher (in the eyes of God) than everyone else? Who are they to think they have the "right" answers above and beyond other global religions and/or other groups doing good things in the community? Many other social organizations and groups do social justice way better than religious organizations. No longer does the church have the credibility to advocate simply because it is *the* Church. Today, we have to earn that credibility.

violate access to human and civil rights). They view Christians as just as likely to cheat, lie, steal, and commit adultery, and think they need religion because they are more likely to do so; this is why they need to go to church each week, to be reminded not to break the commandments. Given these misperceptions, who would want to be a Christian?

Seekers keenly observe whether Christians "walk the walk and talk the talk," behaving in ways that are consistent with their beliefs. When they see behaviors that appear to be incongruent with those beliefs, they question whether members really believe what they say they believe. They understand that practicing one's beliefs can be challenging and everyone will have moments when they just don't feel like doing what Jesus would do, but they expect to be able to see some evidence that being a Christian makes a difference. When they walk into a church for the first time, they anticipate that Christians will make them feel as comfortable and welcome as possible. Yet, because visitors have become such a rare occurrence, members tend to be highly anxious when one appears. They are not always able to control their anxiety, thus making visitors feel anxious.

The disconnection between beliefs and behaviors has led some spiritual seekers to choose other avenues to explore their faith outside of the church. What they are seeking is a context to explore a core set of beliefs. They want to learn how these beliefs will inform their behavior to feel more intimately connected with God and others. They ask questions like: "How can I have difficult conversations with my partner, spouse, children, and parents?" "How do I handle a situation at work when everyone else seems to be caught up in a deception and I don't want to be involved?" "Under what circumstances do I go with the best interests of the majority and when should I not?" "How should I respond to people who are mean, narcissistic, and out to intentionally harm others?" Spiritual seekers are looking for answers that help them improve their patterns of relating to others. They seek to feel more satisfied with their lives by gaining an understanding of their purpose on this earth and how that purpose fits into a grander scheme.

Thus, we need to redefine what it means to be a Christian today. I will suggest that a Christian is someone who has accepted a core set of beliefs about Jesus held by a wider religious community and can articulate how those beliefs influence their behavior (e.g., random acts of kindness and engagement in social justice). By articulating one's faith about why one is doing what one is doing, others will seek the source of our motivation. Just because one has converted to a core set of beliefs doesn't necessarily make one a Christian if one is unable to put those beliefs into practice. One can come to believe in Christianity by connecting experiences of God to scripture, tradition, and reason through worship and Bible study, but being a Christian is about putting beliefs into practice. This is the difference between being a member of a church and being a disciple of Christ.

Discerning a Core Set of Beliefs

The task before us is to determine a core set of beliefs that facilitate this process.[14] By "core," I mean a few sentences which capture the essence of what it means to be a Christian, thus signifying the point of conversion.[15] Core beliefs are the foundation on which we can build the house of other theological tenets. Without this foundation, we become a religion in which "everyone believes what he or she wants to believe." Still, we do not want to make these beliefs so exclusive that adherents come to publicly say they believe, but privately still doubt. Let us not make the focus so narrow that we make people feel like camels trying to make it through the eye of a needle. We should work toward building consensus around certain historically accepted beliefs held to be authoritative concerning the answer to Jesus's question to Peter, "And who do you say I am?" Tradition has held that Jesus is the Messiah, the incarnation of God. Jesus is more than a nice guy, a prophet, and a teacher. Jesus is God in the flesh, appearing to humankind.

These core beliefs summarize what we believe about Jesus's identity. What happens after death, what heaven is like, the meaning of life, and why bad things happen to good people are all theological questions under the heading of "peripheral beliefs." Our core beliefs become the guide for how these peripheral beliefs are thought through and answered. Core beliefs do not change over time and are specific enough to form a religious identity, yet not so vague to be meaningless. These beliefs should encompass the Christian concept of God to determine the church's mission. These beliefs should not be a mere intellectual exercise in critical thinking but should touch the heart and generate a sense of caring about ourselves and others.

---

14. Thriving congregations know what they believe, how they arrived at what they believe, and what difference these beliefs make in their lives.

15. In the emerging church, not everyone who attends worship is a member. Congregations reaching out to their communities may have a number of spiritual seekers in worship who do not yet accept the core beliefs.

The Church's Mission

In 1955, visitors showed up at the door with a core set of beliefs, having been churched elsewhere, often in the same denomination. Today, most visitors come because a Christian invited them. When invited, spiritual seekers will often ask, "So what does your church believe?" They do not want to find themselves in a situation where the religious organization is professing tenets against their sensibilities. The response, "Oh, our church respects that everyone believes something different" enables seekers to continue exploring the spiritual realm outside the church in their backyard. Instead, disciples say, "This is what our church believes, yet we realize that people need an opportunity to discern if these beliefs help them to make sense of their spiritual experiences." By discerning a core set of beliefs, members know how to answer this question. Spiritual seekers should be able to see that all Christians have the same beliefs about Jesus.

The next question is, "Who gets to decide these core beliefs?" Should we ask the theologians at our seminaries, denominational officials, or each local church to formulate a statement based on ancient creeds and historical testimonies? Should we all agree on the same statement of what it means to be a Christian, among all three faiths, Catholic, Protestant, and Orthodox? If each church devises its own creedal statement, it won't take long for Christianity to become an amalgamation of inconsistent and even contradictory beliefs and such an effort will likely contribute to the demise of the church (and not its reemergence). Historically, this has been the role of denominations. Today, however, people want to participate in decision-making. While this may be an extremely difficult endeavor, it may also be an opportunity to bring together a diverse group of people in the Christian church and have a conversation to identify similarities and learn to deal with difference.[16]

What Do We Mean by "Conversion"?

I am not suggesting we act like fanatical, in-your-face, aggressive, "if you don't convert you will go to hell or something bad will happen to you," pushy people who are only trying to get others to join the church to serve their own interests (e.g., to save the organization or their own souls). Most Christians are ashamed of the oppressive, violent nature with which some were converted to Christianity (e.g., the missionary methods of giving money to the poor only if they repented of their heathen ways). Most of us

---

16. Resistance to this project may reveal the autonomy with which many local churches are functioning.

have experienced someone on a mission to convert or change us because they needed something from us. A natural reaction is to be defensive when one is denied access to the power to decide for oneself. Given these histories, present-day Christians (and seekers alike) tend to attach negative connotations to the word "conversion."[17]

In a culture of choice, most people will avoid situations in which others are attempting to persuade them toward a belief system or religious organization. Rather, they look for learning environments to develop critical thinking skills to apply to religious matters. They want to know what the options are, the differences and similarities among global and native religions, so that they can make an informed decision about whether the Christian religion makes sense for them. In the emerging church, "conversion" is not something that is done by an organization to an individual, but a process by which an individual is equipped to have enough information to discern for oneself. The emerging church will facilitate an intentional process to help people to convert themselves. Transformative worship is designed to equip the individual through this process, respecting and honoring one's right to self-determination.

Conversion to a core set of beliefs is not a one-time event in which the worshipper says, "I believe in the apostles creed," but is an ongoing, life-long commitment to learn, discern, discover, renew, and live with the mystery of uncertainty. The point is that these beliefs align with the way in which a Christian behaves toward others. Conversion is not an endpoint by which a believer can say, "I am a Christian" and there is nothing more to do. Some churches give the impression that once one has become a Christian one is "saved" so that they receive a "get out of jail free" card for past and future indiscretions. I realize that becoming a Christian has "saved" some people from acting out their vulnerabilities and helped them to change their lives for the positive. But for too many, conversion to Christianity is all there is to being a Christian.

Conversion is not a gate one walks through or a point of no return guarded by cherubim and seraphim. Throughout our lives, we return to question our beliefs in Christianity, rethinking, fine-tuning, and renewing our faith in light of present circumstances and spiritual experiences. The A to B to C model I have suggested grants permission to return to A and

---

17. By reclaiming the word "conversion" in our vocabulary, we will be more likely to implement the kinds of changes we need to make to the way we worship which will meet the spiritual needs of seekers.

The Church's Mission

revisit the processes of conversion and application so that one matures as a Christian.[18] Helping members to navigate through these two marks along the path of faith formation is the purpose of the church. In this light, we are all spiritual seekers, as we look for encounters to experience God in Christ. All Christians have experiences of feeling as if they are wandering in the wilderness of doubt and dissension. The Church should be able to point us in a direction and give us encouragement for moving forward.

Worship, then, has two functions: conversion and application. The first function is to inspire spiritual seekers to begin the journey to become Christian. This is an observable and measurable result for our efforts of change. A congregation can count how many spiritual seekers are converted to Christianity during a worship service (e.g., by inviting them to come forward for an altar call). Or, they can count how many seekers come a second Sunday or decide to participate in a social justice project in the church. Leaders need to continually evaluate whether worship prepares and equips seekers for conversion to the core beliefs of Christianity.

The second function of worship is to empower those who accept the core beliefs of Christianity to apply these beliefs to Christian practice (which includes ethical behaviors, acts of social justice, participating in rituals, and being part of the process of converting others). Being a Christian influences decision-making and drives a desire to be helpful. Christians have empathy toward the suffering of others, which inspires their work to make a difference in their community. A Christian learns how to talk about what they believe so they can connect these beliefs with behaviors and help others to make sense of their spiritual experiences. Christianity is a religion which is ceremonially practiced in community. It has never been a religion practiced alone in one's backyard.

---

18. Sometimes going back is the only way forward.

Chapter 3

The Function of Worship

Theological Reflection and Emotional Expression

Why do we worship? What is worship intended to do?
How do we balance the thinking and emotional functions of worship?
Should worship be an experience?
How do we convert seekers to Christianity?

THOSE OF US WHO were born into the church, raised in the faith by attending worship, Sunday school, and youth group, have little understanding of what it is like to convert to Christianity (especially as an adult). We became Christian when a pastor sprinkled symbolic water on us and recited the Trinitarian formula. As confirmands, we learned the central tenets of the faith so that we could make the adult decision to affirm our baptism or seek an alternative path (and honestly, I don't remember anyone giving me an option). After an intense journey of education leading to the ritual of confirmation, we were launched into worship or asked to babysit the children in the nursery so the other adults could attend worship. We were not invited to do a ministry or engage in Christian practice.[1] (It's like getting a college degree and not being able to find a job.) And today, congregations struggle to figure out why teenagers and young adults have lost interest in church?

How a religious organization derives its function (what it does) depends on its mission (what it seeks to accomplish). I have identified the

---

1. Congregations tend to equip members for a ministry or practice and then not empower them or empower them before they are equipped.

The Function of Worship

mission of the church as two points along a continuum: to convert spiritual seekers to Christianity and equip Christians to apply their beliefs into practice. In this chapter, I will set forth how this mission can be carried out through two functions of worship: *theological reflection* and *emotional expression*.[2] Theological reflection uses critical thinking to make sense of our experiences of God; it is an intellectual pursuit to know God by studying the Bible and derive meaning. Worshippers develop insights and share these insights with others through storytelling. Emotional expression creates an experience to know God. We feel God's love and thus more fully love ourselves and others. It is an encounter with the tremendous mystery, the awe in "awesome," and when combined with theological reflection produces an *aha*-moment which changes one's life.

Theological reflection and emotional expression are equally important in transformative worship. This is the religious experience that the church has to offer the community. Theological reflection exercises the *head* and emotional expression exercises the *heart*. Whereas some churches focus on the cognitive (thinking) function of worship (e.g., mainline), others focus on the affective or emotional function (e.g., evangelical). Transformative worship seeks to unite the two as a more holistic approach. By creating an "and-both" rather than "either-or" experience of worship, we connect these two aspects of the self (thought and emotion), the impetus for changing one's life. Thus, we need to design worship that is both *spiritual* (an encounter with God in Jesus) and *religious* (the process of converting to core beliefs and the practice of those beliefs).[3] The mind and the heart, therefore, should receive equal playtime.[4]

Shifting the Role of Pastor

For the builder/silent generation, the pastor has been considered the expert theologian by virtue of his or her education at a recognized (accredited) seminary.[5] The pastor's job is to deliver a sermon that convinces, persuades, comforts, and increases the understanding of scripture among worshippers.

---

2. In other words, the goal is to convert seekers and to equip disciples. The objectives to reach these goals are the functions of worship.

3. Christians are "spiritual and religious."

4. Integrating thoughts and feelings is the method to resolving trauma, gaining insight and making sound decisions about one's future behaviors.

5. Preferably a seminary affiliated with one's denomination.

He or she is paid to exegete a biblical passage and write a well-thought-out sermon, perhaps with a few relevant illustrations (and a few humorous ones are good too!). Because preaching has been highlighted as the premier performance of pastors and the sermon is considered the centerpiece of worship, it is not unusual for pastors to spend twenty hours per week in preparation through prayer and writing. All other forms of worship cater to the primacy of the sermon.[6] The competence of pastors is still evaluated by their preaching skills (delivery and content) and whether they can "wow" a congregation. In 1955, the pastor was the resident theologian called by a congregation to preach the Word of God. Hopefully, he or she also possessed skills in pastoral care/counseling, administration, and anything else that needed to be done for the congregation.[7]

The purpose of preaching has been to impart the pastor's wisdom and knowledge of everything religious to those who are sitting on the edge of their pews listening to every word. Whatever the pastor believes about God, everyone in the congregation is expected to believe. Even if a statement seems incongruent or just plain weird, the congregation is supposed to accept this teaching without question: resisting the temptation to filter out what makes sense from what doesn't and reality testing the applicability of these beliefs to everyday living. As a representative for God, the pastor embodies the answers to theological questions and is held up as a model of good Christian living. If another worshipper objects or challenges the pastor's theological premises, the builder/silent generation feels as if their pastor is being personally attacked and may come to his or her defense. They relate to the pastor with a sense of unconditional trust: "even if I don't understand it, the pastor knows better than I do because he or she went to seminary and is an ordained minister."

Respect for a pastor was widely held in 1955 due to a cultural norm toward authority figures. Because organized religion was held in such high esteem, pastors enjoyed an elevated level of reverence (and it was difficult for members to imagine that their pastor might commit an ethical violation). Members were receptive to being convinced of the pastor's theology as the sacred truth. They did not see the need to learn how to think

---

6. To make the decision to call a pastor, search committees want to hear a pastor preach.

7. Recently, some churches have hired resident theologians to serve in the capacity of helping people to do theology. As a pastor, I considered myself the resident theologian.

theologically because pastors were employed to do this for them.[8] The builder/silent generation enjoys sermons with a particular point of view and is less interested in the beliefs of other religions or alternative answers. If the pastor says it, it must be true.

Perhaps as a result of the 1960s rebellion against authority figures receiving free reign simply because of their vocation, the perception arose that "just because someone is in a position of authority doesn't necessarily mean that person is right." Subsequently, the boomer generation began to question the pastor's authority.[9] They still respect the pastor's education and accept that the pastor knows more than they do, but they are aware of alternative beliefs and interpretations. They value the pastor's answers but they also read about religion on the internet to learn about the beliefs of others. They visit other places of worship and pilgrimage to spiritual retreat centers. They may even choose to go to seminary themselves as a second career or upon retirement to study theology. For this generation, preaching is interesting if it doesn't last more than ten minutes, frames questions, explores possible answers, and then makes an argument for the "right" one.

The Gen X and millennial generations are less interested in the answers and more interested in how the pastor (or anyone else who is sharing their faith) *arrives* at those answers. They are adept at asking questions, perhaps because of the freedom that being "spiritual but not religious" has afforded them in casual conversation. To form their faith, they are more process-oriented than their predecessors (who were more content-oriented). While they may be in awe that their pastors went to seminary, education alone does not grant them *carte blanche* to say whatever and not back up their statements by citing the source (so they can check it out too). These generations accept a wide range of answers as long as they are derived from a spiritual experience of God (and they expect the pastor to share one during a sermon). From their perspective, sharing these experiences is not for the purpose of convincing others because people can have a variety of authentic spiritual experiences of God.[10]

Today, the role of a pastor is shifting from being "the resident theologian" to being "the professor of theology." Spiritual seekers do not come to church to listen to others do theology and be fed pre-packaged answers;

---

8. Is the pastor the only one who can pray and read scripture?

9. Today, pastors need to earn the privilege to speak with authority; it is no longer granted by virtue of authorization (i.e., ordination).

10. Millennials perceive there are multiple "right" answers.

they come to church to learn how to do theology for themselves. They want to be equipped with the skills of exegesis, learn the fundamentals of biblical interpretation, increase their literacy of the Bible's big picture, and make meaning relevant for daily living. Transformative worship teaches disciples how to do theology so they, in turn, can teach others. Worship takes on the academic vigor of a seminary class: framing the questions, exploring the options/alternatives, connecting the dots through insight and introspection, examining the conventional/traditional sources, and devising answers which make sense in a particular cultural context or social location. Conversion is a personal decision reached following thoughtful study.

Worship as a Religious Experience

What is worship all about? What is its purpose? Why do we worship God? Is the purpose of worship different today than it was in 1955? To answer these questions, we need to derive a theology of worship; that is, what we believe happens in worship to transform ourselves, our relationship with others, and our relationship with God in Christ. We like to talk about vitality as energy for change and use buzz words such as "transformation" but it is often unclear who we are trying to change (ourselves, others, and/or God). Are forms of worship meant to convince God to come to us or for us to acknowledge the presence of God? Is prayer about changing God's mind to shift the course of history or the minds of the worshippers to adapt to that course? How do we understand what God does in the context of worship? How is this experience of God different from other settings (e.g., hiking up a mountain or walking along a beach at sunset)?

In 1955, people came to worship because of a societal expectation but they also yearned for a religious experience through the pastor's skill at leading worship. A potential member selected one church from others based on several factors (e.g., the pastor's preaching, the location of the building, and warm and friendly church members). Responses to worship were expressed with the following sentiments: "I feel so good after I leave worship. I feel like I can handle whatever comes my way," and "I just love listening to our pastor preach a sermon because I learn so much." People came because they received something useful and relevant to their daily lives. In 1955, worship improved members' quality of life and strengthened their faith in God in exchange for regular attendance in worship, serving on committees, and pledging.

The Function of Worship

While people are still looking for something of religious substance from worship, what they want to give in exchange has changed dramatically: they are looking for an experience that equips them to help others in the church but they feel just as passionately to assist those in the community. They are less focused on maintaining the organization and its structure (e.g., serving on a committee), and are more interested in how the church is making a difference in the community. They want to be transformed by the worship experience to improve the quality of their own lives, but they want that transformation to benefit others. Christian practices such as reaching out to feed the hungry, providing shelter for the homeless, and advocating for the equal rights of all persons, are avenues to put their beliefs into action.

I confess that in most church worship settings, I struggle to experience God. We offer prayers of invocation and sing beloved hymns and listen to the Word from the lectern and the interpretation of the Word from the pulpit, but I don't often feel the presence of Christ through these conventional forms. I realize this might sound sacrilegious, but I have often found it difficult to experience God in the context of a building with formal décor, hard pews, and chandeliers hanging from the ceiling. As a Congregationalist growing up in Massachusetts, I used to love the symbols and icons and statues in the Catholic Church (where I attended worship on Saturday afternoon with my friends). I appreciate the value of these symbolic points of reference to "see" God. I have also experienced Jesus through other worshippers who have offered words of comfort and encouragement at just the right moment. When I pray, I try to listen to what God might be saying. Yet, many of my experiences of God have not been in the context of a worship service.

I am more likely to feel the presence of God out in nature or when witnessing selfless acts of kindness. I see the face of Jesus during meaningful interactions with others. Kayaking out to the middle of a lake and taking in the beauty of the mountains and the reflection of the clouds and the bling of the sun upon the water, I feel God all around me. I am alone without any tech-device, no communication (fearing that if I tip over my iPhone will sink to the bottom). I also see God in the compassion of others. Once when I was in line at the grocery store, a young mother had her bank card declined and the man in front of me paid for her groceries and said he was happy to help her. I experience God every time I have an intimate conversation. When I am lying in the meadow with the wind blowing through the wildflowers and I look up to the sky, I see God. If all worship has to offer is an experience of God, I can find God elsewhere.

Religious organizations do not hold some exclusive claim on God: as if God only appears within the confines of a church or to those worshipping the "right" way. What would a god be like who could only be invoked through certain forms of worship to make an appearance on Sunday morning? Isn't God also experienced in the hospital emergency room, the local bar, and the college campus? Perhaps we should not be monopolizing God's attention away from those who are trying to revolt against oppression and resolve contemporary social problems. Religious organizations point out where they see God acting in the world to bring healing and hope to those who feel broken and desperate. Christianity has never promoted the idea that God can only be accessed in the context of a worship service. God is everywhere.

And yet, worship is an experience. The question is what kind of an experience do we offer to both those who walk into a church for the first time and long-term members? Are they looking for a similar or vastly different experience? As Leonard Sweet has keenly observed in *The Gospel According to Starbucks*, people pay four dollars for a cup of coffee because of "the Starbucks experience."[11] It is not just the product (i.e., a cup of java), but the whole package from being greeted when one walks through the door to the sleek, modern décor and the casual atmosphere conducive for conversation. What kind of experience can the church provide that people cannot experience at any other place? What does the church have to offer to help people live more meaningful lives? What experiences are people looking for from a religious organization?

Before the rise of the "spiritual but not religious" movement, an experience of God was considered "religious."[12] Today, it is more common to speak of such an experience as "spiritual." A spiritual experience is an encounter with God that can happen anywhere, at any time, *and* is not religion-specific. Different religions may interpret these experiences similarly. A spiritual experience does not depend on a particular creed, ritual, or sacred writing to confirm its reliability.[13] Religious organizations function to help people interpret spiritual experiences: to make meaning and assemble

---

11. Another exercise is to ask a group of people why they think people are willing to pay four dollars for a cup of coffee. This helps them to understand what people are seeking from worship.

12. See James, *Varieties of Religious Experience*.

13. Every global religion offers an experience of God. What matters to seekers is the way in which these practices reflect and inform the belief system of adherents.

interpretations into a coherent belief system (faith formation). Whereas a spiritual experience is the work of the Holy Spirit, a religious experience can be planned, implemented, and evaluated. Given this distinction, one can have a spiritual experience in one's backyard but only in the context of a religious organization can one also have a religious experience.

The word "religious" has received a lot of bad publicity lately. It is often used negatively to refer to "organized religion." Seekers have a spiritual experience and bring that experience into the church to discern if our core beliefs are consistent with that experience. The purpose of any religious organization is to function as "a learning environment" to help seekers reflect on their experiences by teaching core beliefs and central tenets based on sacred writings, historical creeds, and testimonies. Contrary to popular usage, the word "religious" does not mean to be self-serving, judgmental, or hypercritical. It means "to connect or to tie" from the Latin *religio*. Historically, the word has been used to refer to a community's interaction with the god or gods. It doesn't serve our mission to become more spiritual within a religious organization. Instead, transformative worship is *both* spiritual and religious: we offer an experience of God *while* learning about the teachings of Jesus.

Diana Butler-Bass suggests an exercise which I have found helpful to make the distinction between the words "religious" and "spiritual." (She uses the words "religion" and "spirituality.")[14] Ask a group of members to generate two lists with each of these words as the heading. Encourage them to freely associate what words come to mind when they think of each category. "Spiritual" tends to invoke words such as innovative, emerging, creative, spontaneous, flexible, etc. "Religious" instigates words such as judgmental, rigid, hypocrisy, stagnation, control, etc. Discouragingly, these are the responses by church members! (When I have done this exercise with college students, I get similar responses.) This exercise helps members become aware of how they have been influenced by cultural forces. We need to revalue the word "religious" to revalue what the church has to offer to the community. If we focus exclusively on being "spiritual," the church will be viewed as one place, among many, to experience God.

What Kind of an Experience Should We Offer?

In worship, I want to *feel* something I cannot feel in any other context. I want to be stirred, moved, challenged, motivated, and uplifted. I carry with

14. See Butler-Bass, *Christianity for the Rest of Us*.

me a reservoir of feelings and I look for opportunities to express them so that I can learn how to more effectively cope, manage, and deal with an array of situations. I long for worship that encourages me to feel angry toward the injustices of the world, frustrated by the insensitivities of others, and accepting of those things I cannot change. I yearn for a place where I can have authentic conversations with others who are also learning about God in Christ. I want to become aware of how I feel so that I can become more empathic toward the suffering of others. If I can change my life, I need a setting which helps me tap into my feelings so I can use them to understand what it is like to be in another person's situation.

Seekers and members alike want an experience of the *heart*. We want to *feel* the wide range of emotions available to the human heart to get in touch with our inner selves so we can connect more intimately with the inner selves of others. We come to worship to laugh and cry, to mourn and dance (and there is a time for every season of the heart). We find few places where people come together and express their feelings. Our society does not encourage people to express emotions (at least publicly) or share details of one's struggles. We maintain a norm which says, "Family problems should stay in the family." We have our Facebook persona, boasting about our travels, parties, and friends, and our inner world of emotional pain that remains hidden from the public view.[15] What if worship became a place where we can be ourselves, sharing our burdens and supporting one another through our trials and temptations?

Worship that seeks to make people happy or lift their spirits becomes "one more place" where people are not encouraged to get in touch with their feelings of sadness, anger, frustration, and discomfort. What makes worshippers satisfied with the worship experience is when they come into the presence of others in a safe, trustworthy environment to tap into their feelings and learn to handle them more effectively (rather than repressing them). After expressing these feelings, worshippers can replace them with different feelings and perhaps change their understanding of a spiritual experience. In this sense, worship can be described as inspirational, joyful, and comforting. There is a line between worship which seeks to "make everyone feel good" and worship which seeks to express feeling to begin a healing process, reconcile emotional pain, and manage the stress of post-traumatic events.

---

15. See Baskette, *Standing Naked Before God*.

The Function of Worship

Worship should also be an experience of the *head*. Worshippers reflect on how they see God moving in their lives and in the world by studying the scriptures, listening to a sermon, and engaging in sacred conversation. Worship should be an exercise in using and improving one's critical thinking skills, stretching one's imagination, and pondering the great mysteries of life and death. Just as important, it should equip worshippers to live with the tension of contradiction, ambiguity and mystery. As worshippers think through the connection between their spiritual experiences (especially those which seem to defy explanation or challenge them to think of God in new ways), they develop process skills (e.g., interpretation, meaning-making, and exegesis) in their quest to become theologians. The premise of theological reflection is to examine these experiences and study their occurrences to be prepared for future ones.[16]

Conversion in Worship

Conversion can only happen in a religious organization (and by organized religion I mean a very broad definition of "community," including groups with a less formal structure than a conventional church). Conversion to Christianity entails a spiritual experience which prompts one to attend worship, to study the scriptures, and to grow in wisdom and in stature and in favor with God.[17] Conversion is both a spiritual experience (God's presence in the world) *and* a religious experience. A religious organization provides direction to learn about the core beliefs of every religion and an opportunity to use one's critical thinking to discern which global or native religion speaks to that experience. When one reaches a point in which one accepts the core beliefs of a particular religion, it can be said one believes in that religion. Just because I believe in the core beliefs of Christianity, however, does not make me a practicing Christian.

In a culture of obligation, the premise of worship was to convince people of a certain theological outlook (and to reassure Christians that their beliefs were "right"). Most members were converted to Christianity by being confirmed into the membership of the church. Worship sought to sustain these beliefs and articulate them (collectively) in the presence

---

16. The Psalms beautifully reflect this theological process.

17. In early Congregationalism, to become a member of a church by confirmation or affirmation of faith, one had to demonstrate that one had a religious experience of God and then studied that experience in order to be able to articulate one's faith.

of God. The practice of being a Christian meant attending worship on a regular basis, contributing or pledging to the financial support of the organization, attending social fellowship events, and being involved in causes promoting social justice. In a culture where most people were Christian by birth, being able to articulate one's beliefs was not necessary for evangelism and therefore not widely practiced. In 1955, the only Christians attempting to convert others to Christianity were missionaries living in faraway lands.[18] Today, our mission field is in our own neighborhoods.

In 1955, being open to learning about other religions or showing any interest for that matter, seemed as if one was being disloyal to one's own religion. If one was truly devoted to Christianity, there was no reason why one should learn about another religion.[19] In a culture of obligation, the key sentiments were loyalty, commitment, and dedication, expressed by exclusively studying one's own religion. The builder/silent generation did not attend worship in other churches, unless it was as a guest for a wedding, funeral, or baptism. Religion was inherited from one's ancestry. Obligation to a religious organization was indistinguishable from loyalty to one's family of origin. Rituals, traditions, and customs (especially around the holy days) are emotionally charged and therefore, were viewed as sacred from one generation to the next.

Millennials do not become Christian because their parents were Christian. Even for those whose parents are practicing Christians, they are curious about studying existentialism, Zen and Buddhism. The cultural norm which says one has to adhere to the religion of one's parents and grandparents is no longer in service. They want to make an informed decision about which religion makes sense for them instead of inheriting religious preference from their ancestors. To make this decision, they may take a course in world religions at college or at a local religious organization.[20] I have found millennials to be curious about everything religious as long as

18. Most conversion attempts today involve convincing the membership to take on a capital campaign to refurbish the organ or repaint the sanctuary.

19. This societal approach to religion has enabled the escalation of international, national, and domestic conflict in the form of prejudice, oppression, and other forms of violence.

20. I recommend to pastors that they offer a course on world religions at their local coffee shop. As long as they stay one chapter ahead of the group, they will be knowledgeable enough to lead the discussion. Discussing one religion each week over the course of eight weeks is a great outreach project, especially for those churches located near a college campus. As a professor of religion myself, we like when a local pastor shows interest in our students.

it is presented to them in a format for expanding their knowledge-base and not to convince, persuade, or assert power so as to decide for them. They want to talk about their spiritual experiences and explore which global or domestic religion best explains this experience in theological reflection. They seek to make their own decisions about religion.

Chapter 4

Assessing Current Levels of Satisfaction

How satisfied is the current membership with the forms of worship?
If current members are not satisfied how do we expect seekers to be so?
How do we change the mind set of the current members to experiment with new forms of worship?

SINCE OUR CULTURE HAS shifted to giving people a choice as to whether to participate in a religious organization and if so which one, worship has become increasingly consumer-driven.[1] Seekers assess if the liturgy helps them make meaning of their spiritual experiences and if the music moves them to feel spiritually closer to God. Parents are looking for educational programs for their children and youth. Members feel frustrated when visitors talk about "church shopping," but in a culture of choice, this is what people do. Members need to acknowledge the shift to a culture of choice so that they will be more in tune with their own religious needs and discern how to better meet them to increase satisfaction levels. Hopefully, then, they will be motivated to meet the religious needs of spiritual seekers. To begin this process, it is important to evaluate the satisfaction levels of the current membership.

If those already sitting in the pews are feeling dissatisfied, it is unlikely that spiritual seekers will expect their own religious needs to be met. Visitors are adept at picking up on the mood of a congregation during worship.

1. We are in the business of converting seekers and putting our beliefs into practice. Our product is accessing emotions and theological reflection. Our customers are seekers and Christians.

Assessing Current Levels of Satisfaction

When that mood communicates, "We are just trying to get through this because we feel obligated to be here," it produces little incentive for them to want to return a second Sunday. Those who have dedicated their heart and soul (and finances) to the life of a congregation deserve to feel satisfied with worship because their religious needs are being met (even if not one spiritual seeker ever shows up for worship). For too long, church leaders' attention has been focused on attracting new people often at the expense of the religious needs of the current membership. Consequently, the pews are filled with a lot of grumpy worshippers.

During my visit to a number of mainline churches, I could feel members' frustration. It seemed to saturate the sanctuary. Sometimes I would find out later they were experiencing conflict over whether to let the pastor go, reduce the pastor's pay to part time, or change the style of worship. Not knowing this beforehand, I struggled to resist taking their mood personally; as if my presence as a visitor was causing a considerable amount of anxiety. I felt their hopelessness and I tried to shake it from my sandals as I left the building. They invited me back the following Sunday (and one time several members chased me out to the parking lot because I didn't sign the guest book). I felt their desperation to welcome "one more member" to do the work of the church. Given this reception in addition to an uninspiring worship experience, I can't imagine why they thought I would want to return.

Assessing current levels of satisfaction serves four purposes. One, it acknowledges that the pastor is not the only one responsible for meeting the religious needs of worshippers.[2] Two, worshippers become more aware of their own needs by participating in the process of evaluation. Three, it establishes a baseline to evaluate the impact of the changes to be made (e.g., the forms of worship), thereby justifying these changes. Because most congregations have no idea what percentage of worshippers are satisfied with worship, this produces a number that can be measured.[3] Four, this assessment allows for a conversation to determine if the congregation feels called to meet the religious needs of seekers and determines their level of willingness to change the ways of worship to do so. The premise of assessing levels of satisfaction is to create a balance between satisfying the religious needs of the current worshippers and those of spiritual seekers.[4]

---

2. Instead, the pastor should be considered the facilitator.

3. Reaching measurable goals is one of the best ways to build momentum in a congregation.

4. I realize by stating it this way I set up a dichotomy between members and seekers.

Doing an assessment assures the current membership that leaders are attempting to meet *their* religious needs *as well as the religious needs of seekers*. Because there has been so much emphasis recently on reaching new people, the old ones are starting to feel a bit neglected, sacrificing their own needs in the pursuit of "saving" the church. Asking members about their own needs can go a long way to making them feel cared for (and members who feel cared for are more likely to care for their community). Asking members if they are satisfied with worship communicates to them that leaders are taking their needs into consideration. We don't want long-term members to feel neglected, betrayed, or abandoned (as sacrificial lambs at the altar of numerical church growth) by leaders who are enthusiastic to get new members. An assessment tool can go a long way to assuring them that their needs matter just as much as the seekers (but not more so).

When we talk about assessing satisfaction levels of worship, most members assume we are talking about the pastor's performance. Once a year, a select group of people conduct a pastoral evaluation to make sure the majority of members are satisfied with how the pastor is pastoring.[5] Some churches send out a survey asking members if they are pleased with his or her preaching, pastoral care (usually evaluated by quantity rather than quality), and administrative ingenuity. If the pastor doesn't rank highly as a general practitioner, this group is likely to call a meeting to confront the pastor and discuss some of the "issues" (and surveys of this kind often don't lead to anything productive). When the pastor hears about the meeting, his or her anxiety rises, wondering what's up and fearing that a group of dissenters are dissatisfied (or just asserting power). When I ask, "Who is responsible for satisfaction levels among members?" the answer is almost always the same: the pastor.

If the pastor gets hooked by the expectation, he or she may override the mission to convert seekers and equip disciples and instead people-please the current membership. When this happens, pastors look toward the membership to affirm their ministry, but they often choose unrelated variables. For instance, if a visitor returns to worship a second Sunday, the pastor looks good but if a visitor does not, the pastor looks bad. If visitors do not show up on a regular basis, the congregation assumes it must have

---

But I do think they have different religious needs and I want to emphasize this point throughout this book as there is a tendency to assume that the religious needs of seekers are the same as members. Yes, there are similarities but it is important to note differences.

5. This small group of people are often referred to as a pastor-parish relations committee.

Assessing Current Levels of Satisfaction

something to do with the pastor's preaching. The idea that the pastor is the cause of mainline decline has become so prevalent in our congregations that many are leaving their vocational calling of parish ministry to seek employment in other settings.[6] The pastorate has become a lightning rod for everything wrong with organized religion.[7]

I find that most members do not know what their religious needs are, making it difficult for leaders to discern how to help other members to meet them. Perhaps driven by a fear of not being able to live up to members' expectations, pastors avoid empowering leaders for this conversation, which only escalates members' frustration. Pastors fear the focus will be on them and their shortcomings (and very few congregations assess the members' contribution to meeting one another's needs). Pastors are usually just trying to do what is expected of them by the congregation. More often, they are doing what they *perceive* to be the congregation's expectations. Conflict erupts when a gap widens between what the congregation expects from their pastor and what the pastor perceives are their expectations.

Not having their religious needs met, more and more members are staying home and becoming inactive. They may not want to talk about their unmet needs because they don't want to hurt anyone's feelings (especially the pastor). It seems easier to just stop attending.[8] When they run into the pastor at the grocery store, they may feel ashamed about their lack of attendance, make excuses, and promise to get back in the swing (even though their good intentions don't lead to action). If they are asked why they are not attending, they may not know. They may say "something spiritual is missing."[9] They may express feeling dissatisfied with the forms of worship, but when asked what the church could do differently to make worship more appealing, they are at a loss for ideas. Very few churches ever implement any strategy to activate the inactive. The lack of effort to assess satisfaction levels with worship is killing the church faster than perhaps any other single factor.

Because the builder/silent generation comprise most of our members in mainline churches who still attend out of a sense of obligation, they *appear* to be confused about why later generations seem less interested in

---

6. In the midst of writing this book, the seminary I attended, Andover Newton Theological School, has just announced they are merging with Yale Divinity School. Fewer people are going into the ministry.

7. Sadly, it is often the members themselves who are attacking their pastor.

8. They assume that they are the only ones who feel this way and so if they go away quietly, everyone else can continue to worship in a way that appears to meet their needs.

9. I hear this a lot from church members who become inactive.

attending worship (as if obligation is still the norm). If one feels compelled to attend worship, satisfaction levels are a moot point. One should go to give God thanks and praise even if to do so is tediously boring. All the better because one shows reverence by being willing to sit through just about anything. I do think the current membership knows why the other generations are not coming but are afraid to state these reasons out loud. (Meanwhile the other generations, who are unaware that there was ever any other culture than one of choice, are trying to figure out why anyone would willingly attend.) In a culture of obligation, it didn't matter much if anyone's religious needs were met because attendance in worship meant one was a practicing Christian.

Somewhere along the transition to a culture of choice, those who attend out of obligation realized they have a choice about the way they worship.[10] Individual members have likes and dislikes with emotional ties to certain forms of worship. Each member also has ideas about what changes need to be made. When the levee of obligation broke, a flood of criticism poured forth (after being suppressed and contained all those years). From the pastor's perspective, it seems like everyone has a complaint about something. After years of attending worship out of obligation and not being concerned about who liked what or what needed to change to attract whom, worship is now geared toward meeting religious needs. What was once a time to be silent (in a culture of obligation) is now a time to speak one's mind in the pursuit of getting one's own religious needs met (in a culture of choice).

Perhaps as a consequence of being silent for so long, members have become hyper-focused on their own wants and desires. Some have reacted to the transition toward a culture of choice, by insisting their religious needs are met, often at the expense of the needs of other members, never mind spiritual seekers. If they don't like praise music because the organist claims praise music is not appropriate church music, then they demand "that kind of music" not be played during worship. If the minister of music plays a praise song against their wishes, he or she may get a check mark against them on a review or the pastor will get a knock on his or her office door Monday morning. Some will argue that until spiritual seekers actually arrive, there is no reason to make changes to the music. But if seekers looking for praise music do show up and the congregation sings three traditional hymns, they may not return.

---

10. Even if they still feel obligated to attend.

Assessing Current Levels of Satisfaction

Too often, those who are the most eager to fill out a survey are those who have piled up a set of presenting problems (and pent up frustration) that they want solved quickly. "At last, my chance to be heard!" What follows is a laundry list of everything wrong with the church, organized religion, and the earth's gravitational pull. Those who perceive their religious needs are being met may be less motivated to take the time to answer questions on an assessment tool. Their lack of compliance should not be interpreted as satisfied. One or two responses in the extreme should not be factored into the congregation's satisfaction levels as they may skew the results and merely be an old grievance. Leaders should be compiling percentile responses to questions so that they can say, for instance, "twenty percent of the responders said they no longer want to sing "Rock of Ages" three times in the same worship service."

Most members are willing to assess satisfaction levels (especially if they perceive this is essential to the process of church growth). The challenge for leaders is to help members balance their own needs with the needs of others (especially spiritual seekers). It should be made clear: we cannot continue to exclusively meet the religious needs of the current membership and expect to numerically grow our congregation. To begin this endeavor, the assessment tool helps leaders to identify the religious needs of the current membership, rate them in terms of most important to least important, and discern the congregation's flexibility to sacrifice *some* of these needs in order to meet the needs of those who are not yet converted to Christianity. The premise of the assessment tool should be to identify what is most important to members and establish the "nonnegotiables," which are not subject to change (although may be slightly tweaked).

Members tend to approach assessments with a renewed sense of optimism: "Finally, we can get things going in a positive direction around here." The tool itself can be revered as the long-awaited savior, promising to reveal the quick-fix secret to turn around the decline in worship attendance. But the tool is merely a way to collect data: it is the prayerful discernment of the data, its interpretation, and the ideas generated that build momentum and the perception of success. All an assessment tool can do is assess. It should not be used to justify firing a staff person or beginning a major building project.[11] Leaders should approach this process by modeling a spirit of curiosity and an expectation that the findings are likely to surprise

---

11. The tool should not be used to do an evaluation on the pastor's competency. There are other tools available for this purpose.

them (instead of confirming they were "right" about something). If the assessment tool is pre-agenda driven, then the answers presumed will be the answers received.

An assessment tool assists members to identify their own needs regarding worship. After they are able to do this, they will be in a better place to negotiate change. Because no one has asked them what spiritually moves them as they worship God, they may not realize there are options. If their needs are not being met, they are likely to default to finding their own reasons for attending worship such as friendships, opportunities to meet neighbors, network for business, etc. They also may feel intimidated about filling out a survey because long ago they surrendered their needs in exchange for these relationships. They may fear that expressing dissatisfaction is sacrilegious or mean-spirited toward the pastor or they will realize just how dissatisfied they are with worship and contemplate going elsewhere. Some will fear the assessment process itself will be like releasing Pandora's Box and all the negativity that has been suppressed will leak out and wreak havoc.

Like other aspects of congregational functioning, leaders ought to make clear the purpose of the assessment tool. "We want to find out what is most important and what is least important to members about the way we worship."[12] This conveys to those who are expected to support and participate in the process of change that what they think and how they feel matters to the pastor and leaders. Instead of navigating around them or pleading with them "to go with the flow," we want them to invest energy and get on board as a valuable resource. Keeping the focus as inclusive as possible gets everyone involved (which we hope will be an outcome of doing the assessment) so that all members work together (synergy). This basic premise of the assessment process should be emphasized: "We want our current members to feel satisfied with worship so that when visitors worship with us, there is a joyful spirit in the sanctuary. We believe Jesus calls us to make disciples, so we plan our worship service to likewise meet the needs of seekers."[13]

---

12. Leaders should emphasize that almost everything is subject to change. The more important a form of worship, the more difficult it will be to change. The tool gives leaders a continuum of what will be the most difficult to the least difficult, depending on what is rated as more or less important. No promises should be made that leaders will not make changes if those changes are only important to a few members.

13. Some leaders will use a threat to get members on board with the process (e.g., "If we don't change the worship service, the church will close"). I have found that the

Assessing Current Levels of Satisfaction

By establishing a baseline of current satisfaction, we can measure whether the changes being made increase these levels. Using the same survey a year later may yield indicators that members are more satisfied with worship, thus informing leaders that the new forms of worship are working. Perceived success generates momentum to make changes in other areas of congregational life. Resistance to change arises because members are afraid that the changes won't produce the desired results (e.g., offering contemporary worship to attract young people to the church and then only current members show up). They are tired of making changes which bear no fruit. For a congregation who feels less confident and has little hope for the future, doing an assessment can interject a sense of enthusiasm by implementing an intentional process to move forward.

It should be noted, however, that when people fill out an assessment online or on paper, they tend to feel as if someone is watching over them. When the moment comes "to speak the truth in love" they may be reluctant to express themselves. The task of leaders is to create a safe environment for the survey to reduce (and hopefully alleviate) members' fears that if others knew how they felt, they would not be considered "un-Christian." Some members hear the voice of an authority figure saying, "If you don't have anything nice to say, don't say anything at all." As long as leaders reinforce their hope to hear from everyone and emphasize that the purpose of the process is to become more faithful to the mission of the church by living out Jesus' commission to convert spiritual seekers, members will feel they can be open and honest about their levels of satisfaction.

Leaders should inform members that just because they are asking for their opinion doesn't necessarily mean the church will make those changes. Leaders are looking for consistent patterns, common themes, and the majority perspective to evaluate the overall religious needs of the congregation. If the membership is primarily comprised from the builder/silent generation and everyone wants to sing "Rock of Ages" three times in the same worship service, then leaders might decide to sing it once instead (and then two hymns from a different genre). The pastor should preach a sermon giving a theological basis for the church's mission to convert seekers to Christianity and equip Christians to put their faith into practice. The assessment tool gives the congregation a starting point to begin this process.

---

congregations that have turned around their decline have embraced a theological reason rather than a threat.

Designing the Assessment Tool

To numerically grow a congregation and attract new people with different needs and interests, congregations identify what they have to offer to the community and what those in the community are looking for from a church. An assessment tool serves to answer these two questions. If the tool finds that members are looking for something vastly different from the seekers in the community, then leaders have a big challenge to balance the needs of both. (But it can be done!) The congregation may need to decide which portion of their own religious needs they are willing to sacrifice to serve the religious needs of those in the community. In the attempt to reconcile the contrast between the two, the first step is to determine what the religious needs are of the current membership and determine how satisfied they are with how worship is meeting those needs.

I recommend that congregations do both a written (individual) and verbal (collective) assessment. For those who do not feel comfortable talking about their dissatisfaction with certain forms of worship (or with the workings of the church in general) the written form can provide an anonymous form of expression.[14] But the premise is to help members develop relational skills to talk about difficult issues and realize that diversity of perspectives is a *good* thing in a religious organization. (It is not difference that divides us; it is the way in which we deal with difference.) Providing multiple avenues to discern the array of these perspectives equips leaders with a broader sense of how people are feeling about worship and determine the range of religious needs.[15] If the written assessment is done before the verbal, members get a sense of what kinds of questions might be asked before they are invited to talk in a group setting.

I suggest leaders ask concrete, practical, and easy-to-understand questions, both yes-no and open-ended with a space on the instrument for an essay answer.[16] Examples of yes-no questions are: Do you think the sermon is too long? Do you think about the sermon after the worship service?

---

14. The issue of whether or not the leaders will assure anonymity will need to be addressed.

15. Individual members tend to assume if worship is meeting their needs, then worship is meeting all members' needs.

16. Vague questions generate vague answers. For instance, consider the likely responses to the following questions. Do you think the church is headed in the right direction? Are you contemplating attending a different church because of lack of satisfaction here? Are your religious needs being met?

Assessing Current Levels of Satisfaction

Would you attend worship if you didn't feel a sense of obligation to do so? Do you prefer an organ as the primary instrument for worship? Would you like to hear different instruments? If the congregation feels called to participate in a numerical growth plan of conversion, are you willing to give up some of your own religious needs? Are you currently thinking about attending another church? Do you think the pastor should be the only worship leader? Should we sing three hymns in worship? Would you want to invite a friend or neighbor to attend worship with you? Are you hopeful about this church's future?

Examples of essay questions are: What motivates you to come to church? What inspires you to invite others to come to church with you? What has happened recently in the worship service that has renewed or strengthened your relationship with God in Christ? What would it feel like for you to sing different genres of music or do liturgical dance? How open are you to change? What has change been like for you in your personal life? Are you willing to allow leaders to make changes to the worship service if it meant converting seekers to Christianity? What is your favorite form of worship and why? What would you like to see happen in worship that leaders have not yet thought of trying? Are we worshipping at a convenient time and/or day for you? Is there a question you would like to answer that we did not ask?

The tool should also ask some more challenging questions, but embed them in the survey. Give the respondent the option to pass over them and offer multiple choices from which to answer one or two. What was happening in worship when you sensed the Holy Spirit summoning you to become a Christian? Which forms of worship help you to experience the presence of Christ? Which Christian practices are influenced by the core beliefs of the church? How does the music make you feel? Would you be receptive to different genres of music if we were attracting other generations into the life of this worshipping community? Which forms, if any, have we been using in worship that feel spiritually void? If you do not attend our worship, what do you think we do? What would you hope to experience if you attended a service? What have you experienced when visiting other congregations that you enjoyed and would like us to try here?

The tool may also include questions that can be rated on a Likert scale (i.e., from very dissatisfied to dissatisfied to no opinion to satisfied to very satisfied), or some version of this rating system.[17] This will produce a

---

17. Likert scale responses avoid the traps of binary thinking (either-or). The con with

statistic (i.e., percentage) that can present a "snapshot" of where the majority of the membership are on a continuum. For instance, if every member of the congregation is dissatisfied with the time of worship and seekers are reporting they do not attend worship because they work on Sunday morning, then leaders have come upon an area to be explored. If every member reports being "very satisfied" attending the small groups where everyone shares what is going on in their lives and how God is involved, then leaders may have an answer to the question of what the church has to offer to seekers in the community. To inspire change and reduce resistance, leaders can make statements such as, "On the survey, 72 percent of the respondents said they want more updated music during worship."[18]

Prepackaged assessment tools are becoming more available and can be found online. The problem with using a "one size fits all" tool is that it is not designed to assess what is unique about a particular congregation (e.g., social location, dynamics, geography) or immediate concerns that leaders are trying to address (e.g., dysfunction, power plays, decline in membership). Religious needs are often diverse and depend on demographics and the cultural environment of the church. Designing one's own tool involves more effort, but if it serves its intended purpose, increases members' motivation for change (as well as getting other people involved), then I encourage congregations to expend energy to create an instrument as a step forward in fulfilling its mission.[19]

---

such an approach is that it is difficult to define these categories in such a way that everyone gives equal weight to each category. Another control mechanism to ensure reliability is to put the same question into the affirmative (e.g., "The worship service helps me to feel connected to God in Christ"), and then later in the instrument to put it into the negative (e.g., "The worship service does not help me to feel connected to God in Christ"). When evaluating, those two questions could be lifted from the instrument and compared (by the same respondent). This technique is also helpful for more challenging questions that are difficult for the respondent to comprehend. The same question can be reframed using different words.

18. If the written tool produces a finding that is prevalent and this is made known, then members may feel more comfortable talking about it.

19. A lack of energy and confidence among leaders to perceive they can design an assessment tool may indicate a lack of energy and confidence to lead deep cultural changes within the church.

Assessment Exercises

To host a gathering to assess satisfaction levels, leaders should select a time of the week most convenient for members (and serve food!) When each member enters the space (and I suggest this be done in the social or fellowship hall), they receive a color swatch and are asked to sit at the table with those who have the same color (so as to avoid everyone sitting with the same people with whom they always sit). A facilitator should be at each table along with a scribe who will record members' responses. The facilitator should tell those at their table that this is not a confidential conversation and that the scribe will be taking notes to share with leaders and the pastor. Who said what will not be identified unless the respondent specifically requests to do so (a pastoral concern may arise). The task is to search for common religious needs. I recommend some training for the facilitators so that this exercise does not become a complaint session (i.e., members look for reasons to be dissatisfied).

Another exercise to assess satisfaction levels among the current membership is to use the bulletin to rate each form of worship. Pass out a bulletin from the previous Sunday to each person at the table and ask them to independently assign a number for each form, such as 1 to 5, representing their opinion from strongly disagree (1) to strongly agree (5). Members respond to the following statements: "this form of worship makes me feel more spiritually connected to God," or "this form inspires me to want to go out into the world and do social justice." The inverse can be used as well: "if we deleted this form of worship, I wouldn't miss it," or "I am often not paying attention during this form." The objective is to discern which forms of worship are equipping members to put their faith into practice.

If a number of forms are dissatisfying, members are unlikely to invite others to worship. They are also unlikely to want to make changes to meet the needs of spiritual seekers (especially those who haven't even shown up yet). If members are dissatisfied with worship, the congregation is at risk for destructive conflict and controversy. It is difficult to motivate people to want to change the way they worship when they attend out of a sense of obligation, especially if they feel dissatisfied and given the choice might stay home. Congregations that have managed to turn around their decline and shift the momentum toward numerical growth are the ones that have been able to have these difficult conversations so they can explore a more excellent way to worship.

One goal of these exercises is to help members to be more open about what they are thinking and feeling with those who care about them. Like witnessing to their faith (a form of worship I will discuss in chapter 6), many will not feel comfortable talking about such personal topics with other members (at least initially). They fear that others will judge them if they speak negatively about worship and/or the church and its pastor. (Spiritual seekers are also afraid of being judged so there may be something to this fear.) Who would want to join this kind of a religious community where people are afraid to reveal their innermost thoughts and feelings? This is one of those examples when the process (engaging in the conversation) is of equal importance to the content (responses to the assessment tool).

With that being said, I wish to pause here and say something to pastors. Please do not take the dissatisfaction levels personally or as an attack on your competency as a preacher, teacher, or caregiver. If you are highly sensitive to this sort of feedback, the members of the congregation will sense this intuitively and rate everything as "strongly agree" (to protect your feelings).[20] You will go home with a smile on your face but the congregation will not have done the hard work to review its forms of worship with the hope of making changes to increase the likelihood of growth. I have seen this unintentional circumvention happen repeatedly. Depending on your comfort level, I suggest you are not present for the gathering session if you might be offended by some of the feedback or if you sense that members are only willing to talk openly without you there.[21] It should be emphasized that this is not an exercise to evaluate the pastor's performance but to assess which forms of worship are meeting the religious needs of the current members.

After all the assessments are completed, leaders gather with the facilitators and scribes to have a conversation about the forms of worship (the pastor may want to be present for this part of the process). Inviting both the facilitator and the scribe allows for a "check in" that they heard the same conversation. (They might have their own agenda and only hear comments that support it.) Responses are reported by the scribe and the facilitator can reflect and clarify. This gives leaders the feedback they need to assess the members' receptivity to change, where some flexibility lies, and which alternative forms members are willing to try. For instance, if

20. This exercise should not turn into a pastor love-fest. If the pastor's self-esteem is dependent upon his or her preaching skills, then the pastor needs to develop interests outside of the church.

21. If you get fired as a result, it was already long in coming and we merely gave your members a forum to have that conversation.

Assessing Current Levels of Satisfaction

everyone comments that the scripture readings are way too long (and I hear this frequently), this group may decide to form a scriptural drama team to act out the reading or simply reduce the number of verses being read or intersperse them with other forms such as music or prayer.

Along with these assessment tools, I suggest that members visit other churches. Doing so helps them to develop empathy for what it feels like when one doesn't know anyone in worship. Visiting other churches also opens their eyes to other forms of worship and helps them to think about why they would want to return to a particular church. I am amazed how few long-term members have ever set foot in another church (with the exception of weddings and funerals) and are unaware about how other churches worship. With this exercise, the member returns with some new and creative forms they experienced in other worship settings. This way, some of the changes being implemented come directly from the congregation (rather than the pastor or a small group of leaders). Visiting in twos allows for reflection over coffee about each other's experience of the worship service they attended together. [22]

I also recommend gathering other groups of people (not members) to discern what they are looking for from a worship service (e.g., lapsed attendees, adult children of current members, and seekers in the neighborhood). These people may not have thought about what they are looking for so should be given some options. Gathering a group of adult children who do not attend worship in this church or elsewhere communicates that the church cares about what they think and acknowledges that they failed to keep them interested (if they grew up in the church). The focus group communicates that members want to reach out in new ways (and it should be made clear that this gathering is not an attempt to try to get them to come to worship on Sunday). I have found that forming a focus group of adult children of current members inspires the members themselves for change. They are more willing to tolerate changes to worship if it means that their adult children (and grandchildren) might attend.

I encourage congregations to gather a group of visitors who did not return a second Sunday. This can be done in a number of different ways. I worked with a congregation who invited all those who had signed the guest book over the past year. They wanted to hear from them why they did

---

22. Another version of this exercise is to ask people to surrender their membership in their current church and go church shopping for another one. Later, they can return to the church and reflect upon why they decided to join one church over others.

not return and if they could have done something differently that might have inspired them to do so. This is not an easy thing to do. As difficult as it is to hear these reasons, the congregation took them under prayerful advisement and because they felt committed to their mission, they worked diligently to make changes. (I was also impressed that these visitors were willing to return to share their experience and be honest.) I have found people are willing to be involved in a focus group if they perceive they can be helpful to the membership.[23]

When We Start Talking About Change . . .

Three issues will be raised in this process. First (and this one usually comes from the pastor), there are forms of worship that are considered to be sacrosanct because of their historical or traditional value for the continuity of Christianity. For instance, most Christians would say, "Worship is not worship if we don't say the Lord's Prayer." Many congregations have updated the language and one might not recognize a translation of the Lord's Prayer (with an effort toward using inclusive imagery). Some members believe that Jesus himself gave us the format as to the way to worship him and any derivative thereof is a sacrilegious act of rebellion (and possible sin). I used to remind New England congregations that at one time in our history, singing hymns was considered blasphemous. In ages past, the saints who have gone before us made these changes to reflect changes occurring in their environment. Changing worship to accommodate cultural shifts to attract seekers to Christianity has been a long-standing practice in the church.

Second, few people are aware of emerging new forms of worship. They make the assumption that we are using the current forms because "that is all there is for worship." When I suggest alternative forms, a common response is, "like what?" Being unfamiliar with what is available to them (in addition to not knowing their mission), they revert to doing things the way they have always done them. It may feel easier to stick with forms that make worshippers comfortable than to try new forms that are likely to make everyone feel uncomfortable (at least initially). For most members, the current forms of worship are all they have ever known. It is easier to remain with the familiar than to wander into the wilderness of the unknown. To move toward transformative worship, members have to be willing to take a leap of faith. For those who have already done so, they can witness about

23. I also recommend paying people for their time.

Assessing Current Levels of Satisfaction

how the process itself inspired a spiritual journey toward a closer relationship with God in Jesus Christ.

The third issue is one of loyalty. Members will answer certain ways on a survey or during a conversation because they want to preserve their relationship with the church, the pastor, and the other members. They have a sense of community, a tribal connectedness and family feeling which all contribute to satisfaction levels (and their experience of worship). The church culture may covertly say, "To demonstrate loyalty we do not say anything negative about our worship service for fear that someone else will be offended." When we are talking about assessing satisfaction levels, we need to take into account that many members will rate their satisfaction levels "high" because they are talking about people whom they love and care about and who have been supportive of them during times of suffering.

Loyalty to pastors is often strong in religious organizations. Members will be hesitant to say anything negative because of a sense of deep respect and appreciation for him or her. (And this is still a good thing as the parish ministry has been so devalued in recent years.) If they rate something low or say anything negative about the pastor they may feel as if they are betraying him or her. If the pastor leaves during the process, they may feel like it is their fault (even if unrelated). Some will fear the pastor will find out how they feel and be ashamed of having said anything at all. Given that the pastor functions as a "representative of God" some members may not feel worthy to judge their leadership in church because it seems as if they are judging the activity of God. At the same time, those who harbor a complaint with God may use the survey to express their anger, having nothing to do with their satisfaction level of worship.

To summarize, leaders are looking for patterns among both the membership and those who are not currently attending worship. An assessment tool is designed by leaders for members. For those with a passion for reaching out, another survey can be designed for those who are seeking something religious. The assessment should be completed by at least 75 percent of the congregation to carry weight, justify changes, and reduce resistance to experimenting with new forms. Being willing to identify and talk about one's religious needs is part of the process of changing people's lives. If those who are already worshipping in this faith community are dissatisfied with worship, visitors are unlikely to return. By increasing satisfaction levels, members are more likely to let go of some of their religious needs in order to become disciples and meet the needs of seekers in the community.

Chapter 5

Interactive Worship

The Flow of Energy and Building Relationships

SEMINARY TAUGHT ME THAT preaching was what good pastors were expected to do well. So in my first church, I invested a lot of energy into producing a well-constructed exegetical sermon. As I stepped into the pulpit, I felt like I was getting onto the treadmill at the highest setting and running as fast as I could, while everyone else came to sit and watch. I did my best to be enthusiastic and inspiring, but when I would catch worshippers yawning it was difficult to sustain that level of energy. I didn't feel like I was convincing anyone of anything, never mind converting seekers to Christianity or stirring Christians to be excited about practicing Christianity. In prayer, I asked God what I needed to change about myself as a pastor and learn to do differently as a worship leader to enhance the flow of energy in worship so that worshippers would be passionate to live as Christians in the community and the world.

What I came to realize is that worship is less about me as the pastor and more about the worshippers themselves and their relationship with God in Christ. Members and seekers alike want to actively participate (and the more active they are in worship, the more active they will be in other aspects of congregational life).[1] The want to contribute to the religious experience of worship: invoking and witnessing to the movement of the Holy Spirit in the midst of joyful people. I observed that it is the interaction among worshippers that generates the flow of energy for praise and

---

1. Sometimes I hear members say, "People today just want to get in and out of worship." I wonder if this is a projection on their part. I begin with the premise that people want to be active in the church; they just might want to do things differently.

worship. Their interaction with one another creates vitality, brings visitors back a second Sunday, and increases satisfaction levels. What the church has to offer to seekers in the community is a religious experience by which they develop relationships with Christians to share what is going on in their lives and identify where God is involved. This is the experience that changes people's lives.

This shift from the pulpit to the pew signifies that it matters who is present for worship.[2] In *Becoming a Multicultural Church*, I testified to the differences between worshipping in a predominantly Euro-American community and one that is multiethnic and multicultural.[3] What I learned from leading this transition is that the greater the cultural diversity among worshippers, the more energy can be accessed during worship. For instance, when each of the generations are represented, the experience is very different than when worshipping with one generation only (e.g., the builder/silent generation). When worshippers from diverse ethnic backgrounds come together and share their traditions and culture, the worship experience exudes energy. Given that God creates us all in the divine image (Gen 1:28), the more diverse the worshipping community, the greater the opportunity to experience the wideness of who God in Christ is among us.

Energy is a significant indicator of satisfaction levels within a congregation.[4] Elsewhere, I have spoken about congregational depression, a condition not unlike the depression that afflicts individuals, draining energy and driving an internal (and often obsessive) focus on all burdens and every woe.[5] Congregational depression is depleting the energy level of many churches today.[6] Members don't want to try anything new because they don't have the energy to implement needed changes, much less the energy to deal with the resistance that will likely arise if they make an effort. To make matters even worse, visitors often sense a congregation's depression long before the congregation acknowledges it. (Likewise, family members often know when a member is depressed before the member can

---

2. In 1955, worship revolved around a worship leader and it didn't matter who was sitting in the pew next to you (as long as you were sitting in your own pew!). From the view of the pulpit, worship leaders saw motionless, expressionless worshippers, casting their gaze toward the front of the sanctuary (affectionately referred to as "the oil painting effect").

3. Bowers, *Becoming a Multicultural Church*.

4. See Crabtree, *Owl Sight*.

5. Bowers, *Designing Contemporary Congregations*.

6. This energy is called by different names. Sometimes it is referred to as "vitality."

acknowledge it.) For members, they have likely become so accustomed to feeling depressed as a congregation, it becomes their new normal.

So let's explore what energy looks like in worship and what leaders can do to maximize its accessibility among worshippers. The flow of energy can be generated on four fields: 1) between worship leaders and worshippers; 2) between worship leaders; 3) among worshippers; and 4) between worshippers who are physical present in the worship space and seekers who are virtually present (via technology). Since the advent of the internet, this fourth field is new for interactive worship, unimagined in 1955. All four fields should be utilized when planning worship. In combination, these fields work as synergy (energy producing a 1+1=3 effect). Each field is equally relevant to create a setting for a religious experience to achieve the church's mission to convert seekers to Christianity and assist Christians to put their beliefs into practice.

Energy Field 1: Interaction between the Pastor/Worship Leaders and the Worshippers

Like a falling tree in the forest, we may wonder what would happen if no one showed up for worship on Sunday morning. Would the pastor still deliver the sermon in the same way as if the pews were packed with people? If the pastor preaches to one congregation and then drives down the street and preaches the same sermon to another congregation does the pastor (and the worshippers) report having the same religious experience?[7] Performers in the entertainment industry rehearse so that every performance delivers the same quality as every other performance. But pastors are not performing and cannot rehearse because their energy depends on the worshippers' level of energy. Unlike actors who attempt to remain neutral, pastors are highly sensitive to the mood of the worshippers.[8] They respond to worshippers' facial expressions, hear the laughter, cry with the tears, and are encouraged by the response to humor and insight or a request for someone to lead the junior high youth group.

Most pastors know what I am talking about. They intuitively sense the congregation's energy level. They may attempt to increase the energy level of the worshippers if it feels waning or become more energetic as the

---

7. The answer is often "no" from pastors who serve two-point charges.

8. A pastor's ability to "read" a congregation's mood is an indicator of emotional intelligence.

worshippers become energized. For instance, when the congregation is in a happy mood, smiling, amen-ing, laughing, and clapping, the pastor is likely to respond by generating more energy. In the same way, bored worshippers can bring the pastor's energy to a screeching halt. As pastors lead worship, they look for signs that the congregation is contemplating the message or is at least on the same page. Those who agree may be nodding their heads and those who disagree may be frowning (at least they are still paying attention!). Some may be daydreaming, others sitting on the edge of their seat listening to the pastor's every word. While the content of a sermon may be written in advance, its delivery depends on those who show up on Sunday morning to hear it.

Traditionally, the pastor has been expected to be the source of energy and the congregation absorbs it like sponges. The pastor prepares and preaches a sermon, and the worshippers listen and ponder its insights. The call to worship, prayers of invocation, and confession are printed in a bulletin or projected from a PowerPoint screen and read responsively between the pastor/worship leader and worshippers or in unison. Worshippers sing hymns, contribute money, and bow their heads in response to "let us pray." To receive communion, they either sit in the pews or go up to the chancel (intinction). In some congregations, unless it is written prior to the worship service, it is not uttered. This format of scripted worship prevents anything from inadvertently going awry.[9] This approach worked in 1955. But today, worshippers want to be part of the action, from preparing worship to participating in the experience.

Systems thinking informs us that the more the pastor over-functions, the more the congregation under-functions. From an energy perspective, the more the pastor invests in planning and leading worship, the less energy is available to the worshippers themselves. Perhaps unknowingly, the pastor attempts to work hard to please the power brokers of the church (out of a personal need to receive affirmation?), leaving the congregation with no other option but to under-function. When I hear statements from pastors such as, "It's easier to do it myself than to try to teach someone else how to do it," I wonder if this dynamic is operative. This unequal distribution of ministry (the pastor doing most of it and the members coming to watch) kept members satisfied in a culture of obligation, but less so in a culture of

---

9. In a culture of political-economic chaos, individuals tend to flock to organizations that provide stability and the allusion of control.

choice. Today, people seek opportunities to be equipped and empowered to do ministry.

In the emerging church, the flow of energy in field 1 is generated from the pulpit to the pew and from the pew back to the pulpit. Transformative worship encourages worshippers to interact with the worship leader (and use the energy that increases its flow in the interaction). Instead of sitting in pews passively, worshippers are invited to move around, express emotion, ask questions, articulate their struggles, witness to the presence of God, etc. Today, worshippers no longer want to be idle observers but active, engaged participants. They can do this in field 1 by interacting with the pastor and other leaders during the worship service.

In my travels to emerging churches, I frequently saw pastors interacting with worshippers. Some asked the worshippers religious questions and they responded with their own answers. This large group conversation was followed by small group conversation to delve into a question further and allow everyone a chance to talk and be heard. Other leaders asked for joys and concerns, and rather than repeating what had already been said by the requester (as if God didn't hear the prayer when said by a worshipper and needs to hear it directly from the worship leader), invited people to come forward and speak into a microphone to the congregation. In one church, the requester then turned and lit a candle before returning to their pew (and this was the most energized I saw this congregation during worship). Other pastors asked worshippers to bring their Bibles and when it came time for scripture, the worshippers read along or read line by line, allowing time for discussion about its meaning (see chapter 6).

Energy Field 2: Interaction between Worship Leaders

Since the decline of available resources, many congregations can only afford to employ one pastor (and many can no longer pay full time). Downsizing puts tremendous stress on one person to access all the energy needed for worship (as well other functions of congregational life) and "perform" well enough to please everyone equally all the time. Pastors often describe the experience of worship as lonely, feeling "on" and judged by the worshippers, perhaps driven by a fear of getting a bad review at next year's annual meeting or on a pastoral relations evaluation. Visitors observe the pastor running around before the worship service making sure everything is in its right place (e.g., the Bible is open to the page for the scripture reading and the sermon notes are still on the pulpit). They perceive that the pastor is anxious about leading worship, which increases their own anxiety in an unfamiliar setting. Alone and the center of attention, the pastor is the mover and shaker of worship and follows the format to a T for fear of being criticized.

For solo pastors, especially for those who feel this way, I recommend investing time and energy to form a worship team. This is one of the most efficient and effective changes a congregation can make to increase satisfaction levels among the current membership *and* increase the likelihood that visitors will return a second Sunday. Forming a worship team shifts the organizational ethos from the pastor as the only servant qualified to do the ministry of the church to an awareness that God calls all members to become disciples of the ministry of Jesus Christ.[10] By inviting and equipping worshippers to become worship leaders, they will become more involved in other areas of congregational life and outreach. When I hear members complain, "a few people do all the work while the rest just come on Sunday morning," I encourage them to pray about forming a worship team. This communicates to the congregation that leaders want everyone to have an opportunity to utilize their gifts for ministry.[11]

Pastors have to be willing to share the spotlight (and the pulpit!). They should manage their fear that others will be able to offer a "better" performance than they do. Worshipping God in Jesus is not a competition to be the "best" speaker, singer, or comedian. I reassure pastors that they are pleasing God when they become concerned they are working themselves "out of a job." The role of pastor will be needed in the emerging church; but what they do is changing dramatically. Today, pastors are responsible for releasing greatness in church members. Creating an environment in which members can be equipped as disciples and develop new skill sets involves taking risks and not being afraid to fail. In this light, the emerging church is appealing to those who want to change their lives. Pastors who feel affirmed because others do "good" ministry, reflective of the church's mission, will find themselves leading an energetic and satisfied congregation.

To form a worship team, pastors need to develop a skill referred to as "indirect success." The pastor invests energy equipping worshippers to lead worship and then empowers them with an opportunity to practice. Pastors

---

10. Members expect to be ministered onto. Disciples expect to minister to others.

11. The number one reason for mainline decline is the under-utilization of gifts by people already sitting in the pews.

feel a sense of accomplishment when a member becomes well-skilled at preaching and biblical interpretation, but they don't boast about it or draw attention to themselves. (They may publicly affirm the gifts of others when appropriate.) Pastors model for members turning disciples, the sense of fulfillment which comes from helping others to experience the Holy Spirit working through them. Pastors who are adept at equipping others to lead worship motivate members for other ministries as well. And congregations that are blessed with such leaders tend to be good at attracting others in the community who seek to change their lives by participating in the congregational life of a church.[12]

In transformative worship, the pastor is still accountable for planning the worship service, but instead of being the "doer" becomes the "coordinator."[13] He or she invests energy into building relationships with worshippers to identify their gifts, talents, and skill sets. (The minister of music should also be coordinating the music ministry rather than being the sole musician.) There is an abundance of resources sitting in our pews every Sunday who, if provided with the opportunity and encouragement, could share their gifts for leading worship. Some are good readers, others can preach and interpret the word, and still others can witness to the impact their faith has on daily living. Some have beautiful voices to sing, others play instruments, and still others dance. Everyone has something to offer as a worship leader but it takes time, energy, and leadership skill to develop this kind of congregational culture.

Transformative worship also extends an invitation to lead worship to people in the community. Those who have a platform or a particular experience to share are asked to lead worship one Sunday. For example, I once invited the local veterinarian (who provided services for many of the members' pets) to talk about what she believes happens to animals after they die (i.e., do animals go to heaven?). She spoke eloquently about her images of heaven where pets and their owners are reunited because God loves all creatures. Another effective speaker is a seeker who may share what it is

---

12. In numerically growing congregations, the pastor did less in worship than in numerically declining congregations, where typically the pastor led the entire worship service. The pastor should do the sermon, lead the Bible study, and bless the sacraments. Almost everything else in the worship service can be done by a lay person.

13. Yes, this is more work for the pastor. It may appear as if the pastor is doing less work if he or she is not leading the entire worship service. Pastors need to educate the congregation that their role is to equip disciples to do the ministry of the church, including leading worship.

like to be on a spiritual journey, to wonder about things religious, and to be curious about whether believing in the core beliefs of Christianity really makes a difference (and developing empathy for seekers is an important practice for discipleship).

As the coordinator, the pastor assesses potential worship leaders for their skills, gifts and passion to lead a particular form of worship. Just because someone has developed public speaking skills does not necessarily imply they will be adept at offering a witness (a story about God's intervention). Instead, this person might be good at reading scripture. Another may have a musical talent and be willing to sing or play an instrument (or learn to play an instrument) but not feel comfortable reading scripture (and most congregations have all kinds of hidden musical talent). Some are good at teaching, some at praying, and some with the children. Together, we make up the body of Christ. Everyone has something of religious value to contribute to the worship experience. They don't even have to be "good" at performing ("good" is subjective) but they have to be confident (as an expression of faith) that the Holy Spirit is flowing through them to create this energy.

Worship leaders serve for a specific period of time, such as a few weeks, a liturgical season, or during a thematic series. The number of times during a given year that a worshipper serves as a leader depends on the average number of worshippers (and some congregations may hope everyone will have a chance to serve as a worship leader). Worship leaders circulate on and off the team (with the pastor being the one constant). For example, if there are four worship leaders on one Sunday and each serves for six weeks, this should be one leader's first Sunday and another leader's second Sunday and so forth. The worship team should represent each cultural grouping in the congregation *and the community* with respect to age, ethnicity, ability, sexual orientation, and economic circumstance. A variety of leaders keeps the worship experience fresh and innovative. By using leaders on a rotating basis, worshippers discover their own gifts for leading worship and doing ministry.

As leaders on the team receive affirmation to generate energy and satisfy the religious needs of the worshippers, they may want to continue past the agreed-upon time limit. Without a covenant for a specific length of time to ensure that everyone has an opportunity to participate, it may become difficult to move one or two leaders off the team (and the worshippers may be patiently waiting for the next group of leaders to circulate). When the same people do the same things over and over again, the congregation's energy begins to wane and others will be less inclined to participate when asked (for fear of taking someone else's job away from them). Meanwhile, those who are the most active in the congregation complain that "a small group of members do all the work." Leaders should recognize how worship enables this sort of behavior when the same people are always asked to read scripture or lead liturgy.

Worship leaders can also interact with one another. For instance, if a congregation is having a sacred conversation about race, sexual orientation, or a political/social/moral/economic issue, two worship leaders can present two (opposing) positions. This exchange should not be staged unless it is made clear that this is a drama, but even then, it gets confusing. Worshippers assume that those who express a perspective believe what they are saying (so essential to being a worship leader as a credibility issue). So the pastor or worship coordinator should find two people who can articulate two sides of a position with clarity, compassion, and conviction. They also need to be able to articulate how that position informs their behavior. These leaders teach people how to have a conversation (process) with those with whom they disagree (content). This process facilitates understanding that there are two sides of every issue. Worshippers can then make an informed decision and be empathic toward others who do not share their perspective.

Another benefit of utilizing multiple worship leaders is that worshippers hear multiple voices from a wide range of perspectives. For a segregated congregation working toward becoming a multicultural one, worshippers become accustomed to hearing different accents and witnessing to the Holy Spirit speaking through this diversity (and come to realize that this is the body of Christ we are being called to reflect as we build the Kingdom here on earth). It makes a powerful statement when there is a wide range of cultural diversity leading worship, proclaiming that this congregation feels called to shift its current composition of worshippers to be a true representation of the surrounding demographics.[14] One strategy to begin making this transition is to invite those from less represented cultural groups (and those historically marginalized from the mainline church) to lead worship.[15] It should be made clear, however, that these individuals represent their own viewpoint on a particular topic and cannot speak for others.

14. For congregations seeking to become multicultural, I suggest instead of inviting people to come to worship as worshippers, invite them to lead a form of worship. Don't wait until someone has been coming for a while before allowing them to serve as a leader.

15. Visitors will assume that worship leaders are in the pastor's inner circle and thus share in that power. When they are of the same ethnic background as the pastor, the assumption is that particular group holds the dominant power.

INTERACTIVE WORSHIP

Traditionally, worship has been about getting everyone to agree with the pastor and leadership. The emerging church does not operate under the assumption that everyone who attends the same worship service thinks the same way about every social/political/moral issue reflecting the stance of the denomination, faith, or religion. (Some denominations pass resolutions to arrive at agreement for the purpose of proclaiming their stance to the wider community.) The goal of transformative worship is not to get everyone to agree. Our mission is to develop a culture where people can learn how to disagree and still be united by their core beliefs about Jesus Christ. Our vision is to create communities where people can engage in conversation, understand both sides of an issue (and articulate an alternative view), and discern which position they should take based on their beliefs and the experiences of others.[16]

In 1955, a sermon had one point of view, derived from the creeds of old and constructed by biblical exegesis. Sermons were delivered by a professional answer-person to persuade the worshippers, who were likely aware of alternative viewpoints with which they may agree, but articulating disagreement was a challenge to the pastor's authority. A groupthink assumed that everyone who was a member of a particular congregation shared the same concept of God as that concept informs social, political, economic, and moral issues. By virtue of his or her character, educational credentials, and denominational authorization for ministry, whatever the pastor believed, all worshippers were expected to believe, especially in matters of theology.

But today we are realizing there are multiple concepts of God circulating in American culture.[17] The emerging church is less committed to forming a groupthink and more focused on granting inclusive space for diverse theological viewpoints. (Tolerance for diversity increases when a congregation has discerned a set of core beliefs.) Worship that suppresses theological difference (even if unintentionally) enables the segregation of worshippers; the greater the similarities among worshippers (with respect to ethnicity, race, socioeconomics, etc.), the greater likelihood of sustaining a groupthink. In contexts where everyone seems to share the same theological outlook and there is little room for rebuttal or space for speculation, adherents actually become more convinced of being "right," consequently

---

16. Instead of mirroring the conflict of the community, the church becomes a place of peace-building.

17. See Froese, *America's Four Gods*.

deeming all others "wrong." Using multiple leaders, expressing multiple viewpoints, raises awareness of other perspectives and assists worshippers to develop empathy for the struggles of others.[18]

Multiple worship leaders also model appropriate and healthy interactions, especially those that are difficult and emotionally charged. For instance, when one is having a disagreement with a family member or close friend, we tend to get stuck in relational patterns (learned from our family of origin or significant others), which may be dysfunctional and dissatisfying. Religious organizations can teach people healthier patterns of relating (and provide space to practice those patterns in small groups). Society depends on the church to teach people how to disagree and to have difficult and sacred conversations. Transformative worship teaches these skills that are transferable to building healthy relationships beyond the congregation.

Multiple Forms Happening at the Same Time

When I was on the treadmill at the gym the other day, I noticed a millennial putting his water bottle and towel on a treadmill three down from the one I was on. He went to the desk, picked up the clicker, and changed the channel of the television in front of him, then turned to the one on the left and clicked to a different channel, then to the one on the right and again clicked to another channel. On one television he watched an update on sports, on another world events, and on still another, a vintage 1970s sitcom. He then started the treadmill and put his ear plugs on to listen to his iPod. At my gym, this has become so commonplace that most people will ask another person several treadmills away if they are watching a television show before changing the channel. And we wonder why millennials find the way we do worship, with one thing happening at one time, so exceedingly dull?

Another significant cultural shift is that we have moved from monotasking to multitasking: from doing one thing at one time to doing multiple things at the same time. We are developing a skill to take in multiple stimuli and accomplish multiple tasks in an abbreviated time span. Few people sit in front of a television any longer without an iPad or iPhone, catching up with others on social media, shopping, or reading a blog. Television

---

18. Religious organizations should help people develop empathy to express compassion for those who may be suffering, oppressed, or victimized. Transformative worship helps individuals to understand what it is like to go through a particular experience or why others feel as passionately as they do about a certain issue.

watchers today are also coloring, knitting, or quilting. When people go to worship and the pastor is doing one form of worship such as preaching, teaching, or praying and all the worshippers are doing is watching, most people become easily distracted and bored with the lack of participation (or at least something to do while they watch). No longer will one form of worship being done at one time produce enough energy for a religious experience.

Transformative worship uses multiple forms simultaneously and in rhythm. For instance, the pastor may be preaching and teaching from the Bible and a musician or band may be underscoring what is being said. In one corner, an artist may be painting, drawing, or sculpting a work of art interpreting the pastor's sermon and in another corner, a dancer is using movement for this same purpose. In one church I visited, each worshipper had an easel with paints and as the pastor read Genesis 1, the worshippers painted each day of creation. One group may leave the sanctuary to go work on a social justice project while another sits in a quiet space for prayer. In transformative worship, not everyone is doing the same thing at the same time and there are several options available for the individual worshipper.

Energy Field 3: Interaction among Worshippers

Many congregations are experimenting with various forms of interactive worship among worshippers. The passing of the peace is one of the most popular forms by which worshippers interact with one another. In some churches, they do not move from their pew and simply greet those next to them by shaking hands and saying, "May the peace of Christ be with you." But in other churches, everyone greets everyone else, with lots of hugging, talking, and lively chatter. Some worshippers report that the passing of the peace is their favorite form of worship while others dislike it for fear of spreading germs during cold season or not knowing what to say. When visiting churches, I noticed that members were warm and friendly, but more so with each other than with me. I felt like an outsider on the rim of a close-knit community as they warmly embraced one another and shook hands with me.

Transformative worship relies on relationships as the instruments by which seekers come to personally know God in Christ. Just like in 1955, people become Christian through their participation in a Christian community. That has not changed. But today, seekers and Christians need to talk openly about their spiritual experiences on the "outside" (the community) as well as the "inside" (the sanctuary). They study the scriptures together to make sense of these experiences, sort through creeds, and embrace historical patterns of continuity. Together, worshippers form and strengthen the faith of one another. Through relationships, they experience the love of God and practice empathy for the struggles of others. They practice what it means to be a Christian when they are able to rise above their narcissistic tendencies and come to understand that Christianity seeks to see the Christ in others.

Therefore, building relationships in a worship service is essential to the mission of converting spiritual seekers to Christianity and equipping Christians to practice what they believe. Individuals often report converting because they saw something in a Christian that they anticipated would make a difference in their own lives. Christians who can learn how to articulate "why they do what they do" as the connective mantra between beliefs and behaviors become disciples who assist others to convert to Christianity. For instance, seekers are less interested in what charity one gives to and far more interested in why one would give away money. Christians do great things in the name of Jesus Christ, but they don't often articulate their beliefs that motivate them to do so.[19] As a result, seekers wonder if good deeds in the community are nothing more than attempts to get people to come to church (or restitution for behaving badly before God).

Small groups are commonplace in emerging churches, but it is cutting edge to use them within the worship service. In the churches I visited, the worshippers seemed to be enthusiastic about their small groups and talked honestly and openly about their lives within them. I found myself talking about things I hadn't thought I would be talking about in worship. While the logistics might be a little complicated (especially when the sanctuary has unmovable pews), worshippers seemed willing to adapt to have these conversations. I envision transformative worship being a combination of large group worship in a sanctuary and small group worship for relationship building. Worship is where people can share what is going on in their lives and discern where and how God is involved. Church is one of the few places in our society where people feel free to be themselves and find the support they need to manage life's challenges with dignity and grace.

---

19. One congregation asked members to spend a liturgical season paying for the car behind them in the fast food line and leaving a card about the church with the cashier at the window. Seekers want to know why Christians do random acts of kindness (although they also appreciate free food!).

Energy Field 4: Interaction between Worshippers Actually Present and Those Virtually Present

The trend still continues to either have all worshippers in the same actual space for worship or to hold worship on the internet where everyone remains in their own home. Some churches, however, are now using technology to live stream their worship service. Putting one's worship service on the internet (either live or to be watched at a later time) helps Christians to reach a wider group of seekers, who may or may not live close enough to the church to one day actually visit. Too often, leaders resist the idea of virtual worship because they claim it's not personal enough, but that can also be a matter of perspective. Let those who are seeking decide the level of personal interaction that feels comfortable for them. They can also see how members interact with seekers in the service before they decide to visit.

For those who are not physically able to attend worship, especially those in the builder/silent generation who have had long-term relationships with other members as well as the setting, they can now "go to" a worship service. Previously, if a member was ill, physically or emotionally restricted to home, working on Sunday morning, or just too busy, they would miss attending worship. For some, virtual worship may not be the same as attending in person or an acceptable substitute, but it is an option previously unavailable. Today, those who are unable to be actually in the sanctuary can watch, participate, and interact through their computer. Unlike their parents, who once they became "homebound" could no longer attend worship, present-day generations will continue to worship via technology.

For seekers who are hesitant about walking into a religious organization because they do not know what to expect, they can attend a worship service online to get a sense of the experience to discern if this church may be able to meet their religious needs. Virtual worship can take the fear factor out of attending for the first time as they watch several services and then decide whether to visit. In virtual worship, they can see the space, observe what the pastor does, and note how the congregation responds. They can also become familiar with the forms of worship. Seekers look for these experiences on the internet, sometimes for convenience, other times just out of curiosity. Virtual worship may prove to be one of the most effective strategies for evangelism/invitational ministry in the twenty-first century.

The cell phone is another device that the church can use to reach out to spiritual seekers. When worship leaders request all worshippers turn off their phones so that they do not ring during the service, the millennials don't know how to do this (even airlines no longer require phones to be set on airplane mode). For transformative worship, leaders ask worshippers to take out their phones and text someone about something that just happened in the service: an experience of God, a meaningful moment, the work of the Holy Spirit, a personal transformation, or a conversion to Christianity. The phone is a great link between those in the sanctuary and those online. I heard one pastor say, "Will everyone please text someone they know who is not here and tell them what we are doing or send them the following message." Why would we want to ask people to put away a connector between ourselves and potential members?

This field is the least utilized and yet holds the most promise to inspire those who have little interest in organized religion to attend a worship service. As members are being equipped to make disciples, they are realizing that we need to use technology and the internet for this mission. No longer can we put catchy religious sayings on signs or "everyone is welcome here" and expect visitors to show up. Using all forms of social media, such as Facebook, Twitter, and Instagram are all the current craze (and will probably be passé by the time this book is published). How do we use these avenues to practice invitational ministry right from the comfort of a well-padded pew? We invite worshippers to turn on their technological devices and connect with the virtual world. In time, we will come to appreciate that the iPhone is God's gift for evangelism in the emerging church.

Chapter 6

Faith Sharing and Formation
Witnessing, Small Groups, and Bible Study

WHEN MY DOGS RAN out of heartworm medication, I called the veterinarian. Because it had been eleven months since their last visit, he had to give them a heartworm test before renewing the prescription. Annoyed about the inconvenience, I brought the dogs to his office at the end of the day. While in the waiting room, a woman came in with an old looking husky. He plopped to the floor beside her and rested his tired muzzle on his paws. He looked like he had chewed his last bone and chased his last ball. Suddenly, the woman burst into tears. Another dog owner sitting close by asked why she was crying. She explained to the room full of heartfelt listeners that the purpose of the visit was to let her dog go to doggy heaven. As tears rolled down her face, she reflected on all the good times they had together. By now, we were all crying with her. Someone passed Kleenex tissue around the room. A group of strangers found themselves offering sympathy and support to one mourning the loss of a significant other.

It was more "church" than I had experienced for some time.

I fail to understand why so many religious organizations do not support a culture where people talk about religion. When seekers walk into a church, they wonder why the pastor is the only one who shares his or her faith and everyone else is expected to remain quiet. For those who are used to religious talk elsewhere, they come anticipating there will be lots of religious talk, given that they are in a religious context. If this doesn't happen, they may seek out another church-related venue (e.g., a potluck dinner to see if people talk about religion there). Yet, most church events are geared toward socializing rather than talking about religion. Spiritual seekers do not need another place where people do not talk about their faith; they already work for a corporation or attend an educational institution where the subject of religion is off limits. Therefore, they seek out places that offer meaningful conversations about religion. They are confused why the church would not be one of those places.

Most of us have had a significant, life-changing, awe-inspiring experience when something happened and we wondered if it was divine intervention; that is, the work of the Holy Spirit, an encounter with the face of Jesus, or a miracle at the hand of God. Someone showed up at just the right moment or said the right thing to make us reflect and change our course of action, making all the difference. After a long hike up a mountain, when we reach the summit and behold the magnificence of creation, from the lakes and clouds, the valleys and plains, we wonder what life is all about and how we fit into the grand scheme of the Creator. There are also times when we reached a point where we felt we could go no further and someone brought us hope and healing to take the next step. These experiences are beyond coincidence and summon us to wonder about the mysteries and uncertainties of life. How does Christianity (as a set of beliefs and practices) help us to understand these spiritual experiences?

Seekers are enthusiastic to talk about their spiritual experiences and they do so in cafes and bars; they enjoy gathering with friends over a latte or libation. They wonder what happens in a church to suppress one's natural curiosity about everything religious and they fear if they attend that the same thing might happen to them. They know the human spirit possesses an inherent need to understand spiritual experiences in the pursuit of making meaning (which often helps us cope with suffering). Prayer and meditation bring one only so far on the journey until we want to bounce ideas off others who affirm and challenge our perceptions (so we can grow in faith). In the company of others, we express our emotions and feel understood. These conversations help us to emerge from a crisis with a renewed sense of confidence. We are created with a longing to be in community to share our joys and sorrows as we support one another through our adaptive challenges.

For those who were spiritual seekers before converting to Christianity, they may have had to sacrifice talking about what they really believe in order to become a member of a church. One of the reasons why they were excited about attending worship is the opportunity to talk about their spiritual experiences. When they are unable to do so, or worse, discouraged from doing so, they may feel disappointed. In order to fit in and feel like they belong, they assimilate to the church's culture by refraining from talking about what they believe and guarding against sharing too much information about their personal lives. They learn that to become an official member of a church, they are expected to show up for worship and pledge. Conformity to the status quo too often requires accepting a collective groupthink. In time, they lose their luster for talking about religious matters.

This expectation of silence means that most members have not given much thought to this subliminal by-law. It wasn't like a committee sat around a table and decided to invent a church where only one paid person could talk about his or her faith and everyone else would be expected to agree or remain quiet. "It's just the way we've always done it." But we continue to enable a cultural expectation in which the level of personal sharing is kept to a minimum (e.g., reserved for a major crisis or loss when prayers are requested). When I suggest doing things differently, most members look bewildered and inquire, "Are we allowed to change things?" Others ask, "Like what?" fearing I will suggest something so out-there it will sound sacrilegious. Still others hope I will offer new ways to worship which will interject a spirit of enthusiasm into an otherwise dreary format. Like seekers, members yearn to share their personal lives and talk about their faith; they just have never done it that way before.

Given their unfamiliarity with this practice, members may approach personal sharing with fear and trembling. They have been taught that religion is a private matter like family problems. This norm is so embedded in the culture of most of our churches that inevitably someone will respond to my ideas by saying, "Personal sharing may go over in another region of the country, but not around here" (and I hear this often!). They default to their ethnic background (e.g., German) to justify their resistance to making worship more personal. I have learned that part of what this resistance is about is the fear of being judged. They are afraid of feeling exposed and others not liking what they see. Because the builder/silent generation has a deep desire to belong to organizations (and not feel ostracized from them), it is a huge risk to be transparent in a setting where they have learned to keep up appearances by dressing nicely and treating others kindly.

I have learned that it only takes a few members to have a positive experience in a small group or hear a witness by a worshipper in another church to set the stage for change within one's own congregation.[1] For those who have already instituted small groups in other contexts (e.g., adult education), it may be easier to begin using them in worship. Some may resist trying small groups during worship because they do not want to lose their small group in another setting. If they can articulate this fear, which is affirming of their small-group experience, they will make others curious and more willing to experiment with small groups. When a few members are excited about a new form of worship, they likely will convince others to at least give it a try. When a few cast such a vision, even those who may be hesitant may tolerate these changes to worship, even if they do not want to participate (and this should be an option).

Witnessing/Testimony

When I speak at events, I am often asked "If you were going to recommend only one change to the way we worship, what would it be?" I answer "witnessing." When I look back on my experience of leading numerical growth in four congregations by transforming members into disciples, witnessing was the most effective change we made to worship in order to fulfill our mission. When one witnesses, it is a visible indicator that a congregation is making the transition from functioning as a pastor-driven organization to one which is Holy Spirit–driven by disciples. When we asked visitors why they returned a second Sunday, they responded that they identified with the person who had witnessed the previous Sunday. As one witnessing told their story, seekers saw themselves in a similar struggle and found hope. Visitors would say, "If that person could make it through their crisis with the help of God, then I have faith God will help me make it through my own."

Congregations numerically grow when members, turned disciples, begin inviting others to come to worship.[2] Witnessing creates a culture in which people can be authentic, revealing who they are (the good, bad, and ugly), and envision who they hope to become. Disciples want to share what they are experiencing in worship with friends and family. For years, I encouraged, (heavy sigh) begged members to invite others to attend worship but very few ever did so. Some tried to invite others, "Do you want to come to worship

---

1. This is another reason why I encourage members to visit other churches to experience different forms of worship.

2. As members become excited about their ministries and what is happening in worship, it is easier for them to invite others.

with me?" but the answer was usually "no." I learned that seekers need an invitation that involves sharing one's faith.[3] To help members talk about what they really believe, witnessing in worship becomes an opportunity to develop their discipleship skills and feel confident as invitational ministers. By participating in the small groups and witnessing, members learn how to talk about their faith. They are then equipped to do so in other settings. When members are able to talk about what it means to them to be a Christian, it isn't long before visitors begin appearing at the door.[4]

As a pastor, when I first introduced the idea of witnessing, there was an aura of awkwardness in the air. People didn't know what to say when they witnessed. They feared saying too much and feeling exposed and ashamed or sharing too little and being accused of lacking faith. They stumbled over words, became emotional when they didn't expect to be, shook uncontrollably when they got nervous, and became incoherent when they lost their train of thought. And yet, they persevered with tremendous grace and dignity. They made us laugh and they made us cry. They provided us with a sense of hope that if God had intervened in their situation, God will intervene in our own. Witnessing became the centerpiece of the worship experience. When worshippers were asked on a second round of surveys about satisfaction levels, leaders noted a significant increase. They were now excited about being in worship. They were hearing stories from other members who had sat next to them in the pews for years.

Not everyone caught the vision. One of the youth ministers used fifteen minutes to express her frustration toward the congregation for not adequately supporting the youth ministry program (at least by her standards). I was summoned to a Christian education team meeting after an openly gay man talked about what it was like growing up gay. (Some of the parents were asked by their children on the way home what he was talking about.)[5] One group of parents wanted their children present for witnessing and another group of parents felt it was not appropriate for children. (Sometimes you can't win!). Initially, a few members thought we were doing "bios" from the chancel "to get to know each other better," and began by saying, "I was born in 1972 . . . " (Everyone hunkered down for a long, drawn-out life-

---

3. See Bowers, *Invitational Ministry*.

4. Those who have recently converted to Christianity are often the best evangelists as they are able to talk about how their lives have changed since becoming a Christian.

5. This might have been an opportunity to discuss the subject but the parents who were angry did not perceive it that way.

summation.) Like anything else new to the worship experience, witnessing came with its kinks. In time, thankfully, worshippers adapted to the challenge and became skilled at this Christian practice.

I introduced witnessing to the congregation by asking twenty worshippers (both spiritual seekers and Christians) to each witness over the next twenty weeks (one per Sunday). I selected these people based on three criteria: 1) those who had a recent crisis or trauma and had asked questions such as, "Where is God involved?" "What is God doing to help me to help myself?" "How can I use this event to be more helpful to others going through a similar event?"; 2) those who were able to express emotion and articulate how this event contributes to forming their faith (even if they doubted); and 3) those who held some status in congregational life.[6] I devoted energy to equipping these twenty so that they could teach other members how to talk about a spiritual experience and point to how the church helped them to form and strengthen their faith. The selection of the first twenty sets the stage for what witnessing will be like in a particular congregation.

What I didn't see coming was that because the first twenty people were so good, everyone else was afraid to follow them. I had to remind the congregation that we are not here to compete with one another for who wins the best witnessing category, but to give God glory. Witnessing is not a contest for disciple-of-the-year. Even the first twenty were afraid of not being "good enough," and a few refused my request for fear of disappointing me (which was more of a problem with my leadership). I kept repeating the assurance that witnessing is not a performance to be judged, but a means to invoke a religious experience. Granted, not everyone is a good public speaker, but everyone has a good God-sighting story. Even those who did not speak eloquently could testify to the power and promises of God in Christ and in so doing, bring hope to someone else.

I also spent some time casting a vision for how this new form of worship contributes to our mission. This helped the first twenty prepare what they were going to say. Some wrote down every word and read from a manuscript. Others referred to an outline. Some were more spontaneous and didn't know what they were going to say until the moment they spoke. I didn't insist on one style over another as long as the one witnessing

---

6. This criterion might come as a surprise to the reader. But when beloved church members who held some influence in the church witness, it convinced members to be more willing to try something new even if it made them feel uncomfortable.

had some self-awareness about which style helped them to communicate their message most effectively. Some worshippers perceived that those who witnessed from a manuscript were "better prepared" than those who spoke without one, while other worshippers complained that those who had a manuscript were just reading it without much affect. I did not check in with them beforehand to inquire what they were going to talk about, trusting in their relationship with the Holy Spirit. This involves a leap of faith by pastors, because whatever they put out there cannot be retrieved.[7] It's like toothpaste: once it's out, you can't get it back in the tube.

Witnessing is not a pity party nor an attempt to make others feel guilty or ashamed. Too many sermons talk about how the pastor saw Jesus in the face of those imprisoned and too few teach prisoners how to see the face of Jesus in one another. Witnessing should help worshippers resist the tendency toward narcissism and arrogance and manage their selfish desires. It is not an exercise in boasting or self-promotion. In a culture that frames most motivation in terms of "what's in it for me?" witnessing communicates the personal value of being compassionate and generous to others. Because disciples are called to help others and make a difference in their community, witnessing identifies what people need (rather than guessing) and responds in kind. Developing empathy motivates people to want to help others to change their lives.

Despite several learning curves, we had great success with witnessing, especially to help people change their lives. Some who witnessed talked about depression, the dark night of the soul, feeling helpless, cheated, and desperate. They talked about how the church helped them to have a relationship with Christ and how this did not cure their depression but helped to manage it better. Those who were in Alcoholics or Narcotics Anonymous tended to be really good at witnessing because public sharing is encouraged by the culture of these organizations. We had witnesses reveal they were victims of childhood abuse and spoke of how this trauma affected their concept of God. We heard about how a crisis tends to either strengthen or weaken one's connection with God and learned that the turning point involves making an intentional choice (a consistent theme). Worshippers began to identify factors to strengthen their relationship with God in Christ. They also realized

---

7. The pastor should make clear to the worshippers that they do not know what will be said by the one witnessing. This way, the one witnessing should be responsible for what is said.

everyone has a story that would break your heart. This insight inspired them to practice random acts of kindness, even to strangers.[8]

These are responses to hearing a worshipper offer a witness.

"I had never thought about it before; that the Holy Spirit is helping me to help others. I realize now that I have been focused on myself and my own wants and needs. Yet, when I focus on someone else, those yearnings are fulfilled."

"I really identified with her story as I am going through a similar experience; her story helped me to rewrite a happier ending because she helped me to see I had other options."

"I've never cried with a community of people before. It was so sad when she was telling her story. As she relived these events, this time we were there with her and could help her to realize that it wasn't her fault and that she could now put the experience in a different perspective."

"I had never imagined what it was like to have others treat you a certain way because of one's ethnic or racial background. Hearing these stories made me understand that when I do nothing, I am enabling these social problems. I am now realizing I have some of my own prejudice to deal with."

"The next time I see someone homeless on the street, I will look at them differently. After I heard that homeless man talk about his faith, I feel like I can handle just about anything."

"I didn't know what to make of what happened to me. But when I came to church and heard the story of how Jesus healed the blind man, I realized that Jesus is healing my blindness."

"I sat next to her in the pew for twenty years and had no idea she had been through such a horrendous experience."

"The one witnessing told a story about why he no longer believes in God because he thought God had abandoned him in his time of need. But I could see God throughout his story."

---

8. In the multicultural, multiethnic church where I served as senior pastor, hearing stories of oppression and violence helped people to confront and confess their own prejudices and become active in the community to alleviate racial tension. As people shared their stories, others recognized how they were supporting the oppressive structures which caused and contributed to their plight. They were empowered to leave worship and go out to do something to effect change in the community. The more worshippers heard and understood the struggles of others, the more they to put their faith into Christian practice.

Not every story has to have answers nor specifically witness to God's presence. Some of the most powerful witnessing was by people who went through a crisis and could not find God anywhere. They expressed feeling rejected and abandoned by God or worse, punished for a past indiscretion. The other worshippers seemed to be drawn into the story to figure out where God was working behind the scenes or in the margins. Some talked about how they lost faith years ago but didn't feel safe to tell anyone within a church for fear that others would judge them in a negative light. Spiritual seekers are grateful to those who are willing to admit they doubt or do not believe everything that has been historically touted by organized religion. These are moments of authentic sharing and it is through these moments that spiritual seekers convert to Christianity.

What are spiritual seekers looking for? They are looking for a religious community where worshippers can talk about what they really believe and not be afraid of others judging them or calling them names such as "un-Christian" or threatening them with the ravishes of hell. They are looking for a place where they can share their stories, listen to the stories of others, and discern the work of the Holy Spirit. They want to know what it means to be a disciple of Jesus (a Christian) and the value that being a Christian makes in everyday life. They are looking for a group of Christians who will challenge them to improve the ways they relate to their loved ones and those they do not know yet. Seekers are looking for a community of faith where everyone is on a journey and willing to walk together to help each other to see God along the way.

Small Groups

Many congregations are also using small groups to create space for building relationships and personal sharing. This has come about not so much for the purpose of attracting seekers, but because members themselves are looking for opportunities for meaningful interactions. While they have known other members for years, they may not have had an opportunity to talk about their faith and its formation through their own spiritual experiences. When asked about what they believe, they may not be able to articulate these beliefs because they have not developed the skill of talking about their faith and may lack the confidence to do so with conviction. A benefit of small groups is that they provide a setting for Christians to learn how to speak about their beliefs. Even though initially members may feel uncomfortable talking about what is really going on in their lives (remind them that they are doing so with people who love and care about them), small groups provide a setting to practice being a disciple.

Another benefit of small groups is that they give seekers and Christians a structured forum for conversation between each other. Seekers listen to Christians talk about how important being a Christian is in their lives: how they find strength and courage in their relationship with Christ. Christians listen to seekers talk about their spiritual experiences. Small groups bring together diverse people who are unlikely to interact in any other setting.[9] In our society, there seems to be a natural tendency for "like" people to flock together (e.g., Christians hang out with other Christians, seekers with other seekers).[10] Small groups interject some intentionality into the interaction between the two. Christians are not only helping seekers to convert to a particular religion, but this process also helps Christians to put their faith into practice (thus mutually beneficial to both). Without the presence of seekers in a worship service, Christians are not fulfilling their mission.

Some churches are already using small groups in their community life (e.g., adult education). This setting gives members an experience in sharing their faith. For those seekers who may be hesitant about attending a worship service, attending a small group instead gives them a chance to develop relationships with members, ask questions about what Christians believe and get an overall sense of what a religious experience is like. Some small groups focus on interests (e.g., quilting groups), while others are crisis-specific (e.g., support groups for those with cancer or those experiencing a major loss). Small groups introduce seekers to the Christian faith. They also help seekers to change their misperceptions about "religious people" as judgmental and inflexible. After attending a small group for several months, they may show up at a worship service.

Some congregations are experimenting with small groups *within* the worship service. While the logistics of this might seem a little complicated, they don't have to be so. (And the Bible does not say that the only way to worship is to sit in a pew facing toward the chancel.) To design a worship space that supports small groups, a congregation may prayerfully consider removing the church pews and purchasing moveable chairs (see chapter 9).

---

9. When members are asked why they don't invite seekers, they will often say, "Because all my friends already go to church." Jesus doesn't call us to befriend those who are already Christian, but to reach out to seekers.

10. This is true in the church as well. Note who drinks coffee together during fellowship hour.

Faith Sharing and Formation

If this is not an option, small groups can still be used as a form of worship with pews or worshippers can move to Sunday school rooms or sit around tables in the fellowship hall. Initially, this may feel awkward right in the middle of the worship service. Pastors are often concerned that physical movement will break the flow of the worship service but it may help members to refocus their attention when they return to worship in the sanctuary (kind of like a seventh inning stretch). Hopefully, when pastors hear positive feedback about the experience of moving around during worship, they will appreciate its value.

Prior to moving into the small groups, the pastor or worship leader may assign a topic for discussion. This can be done by posing a question and possibly giving an array of answers for exploration and discussion. Or, worshippers can be sent forth to talk about their faith and a recent spiritual experience they are trying to understand. After experimenting with different options, leaders should assess if this worshipping community prefers more or less guidance for topics to encourage faith-sharing. It is likely that a leader will arise in each group to facilitate the conversation, but sometimes these leaders are self-appointed and have their own agenda which can disrupt the process. By giving a specific topic, others can redirect by saying, "Let's get back on track. We were asked to talk about the following . . . " Yet, the group may sense that someone needs to talk because they are struggling with a current issue and so decide as a group not to address the topic. We don't want to feel as if the small groups are micromanaged by the worship leaders, but we also don't want them looking at each other not knowing what to say.

I suggest leaders derive two sets of questions for discussion in the small groups. The first set are for those groups where worshippers do not yet feel comfortable talking about their faith. When the congregation first experiments with this new form of worship, they may need time to become accustomed to what is expected from them. Leaders should provide a rationale for the two sets of questions so that worshippers don't feel they are being asked to do something that is stretching way beyond their comfort zone. The second set of questions are for those who are skilled at talking openly and trust others not to judge them (or can confront those who do judge them). The goal is to blend these groups so that those who feel comfortable put others at ease.

The first set of questions might include the following: What is your favorite Bible passage and why? What was your favorite memory of church growing up as a child? What has been your experience since? Who was your favorite Sunday school teacher and why? If you have never been to church before, what did you think it would be like? What do you think is the most religious show on television?[11] Do you believe that God calls people to particular professions? If so, what do you do for a living? What would you like to talk about?

The second set of questions might include the following: What do you believe happens after one dies? What do you think heaven is like? Have you lost someone close to you? What was that experience like for you? What is the meaning of life? Why are we put on this earth? Why do bad things happen to good people? What does the Bible say about how we are supposed to live our lives? What do you find to be the greatest challenge of the Ten Commandments? Have you experienced a God-sighting recently? How did this experience change your life? What do you think God is like? What is the relationship between God, Jesus, and the Holy Spirit? What is your favorite story that Jesus told? What parable has helped you to take the high road when someone was mean to you? Is anyone in our group experiencing a personal crisis that they would like to talk about?

As the congregation becomes accustomed to small groups during worship, they are invited to move on from the first set of questions to the second. Eventually, they may want to do a "check-in" when each person in the group shares what is going on in their lives and where they are struggling with their faith. Small group participants minister to each other and identify the presence of God to make a difference in their lives. Most visitors who attend worship for the first time are experiencing a personal crisis and look toward a religious organization as a place to receive comfort, support, and insight. Small groups grant them a sacred space to talk about the crisis and receive the immediate support they need (and a member can follow up or ask permission to bring their need for care to the attention of the pastor). When we create settings where people can be themselves and share their burdens, they are likely to return a second Sunday.

Bible Study

Since the Reformation, the Bible has been upheld as the sole source of authority (for Protestants) to answer theological questions, to identify what it means to be a Christian, and to determine how the church should function

11. My answer is *The Simpsons*.

with respect to mission and vision. Prior to the Reformation, worshippers could not access a Bible and were dependent upon educated clergy to read, translate from the original text, and interpret its meaning. The Reformation inspired a desire among all Christians to study scripture and to learn how to apply its relevance for daily living. *Sola scriptura* was granted authority over the other three sources of reason, tradition, and spiritual experience. To determine whether someone had a *significant enough* religious experience for conversion (so that they were *allowed* to join the church), they turned to the Bible to see if scripture supported their experience; providing a frame of reference to make meaning of that experience.

In 1955, spiritual experiences were considered the lowest source of authority (i.e., the least reliable). Today, they are increasing in their authoritative value, especially among seekers. For some, spiritual experiences rank above the other three sources.[12] Seekers may be cautious about sharing these experiences for fear they will be dismissed by members. This is what the "spiritual not religious" movement is about: the premise that people can have spiritual experiences of God outside of the church that do not need to be explained or validated by the church. In the eyes of seekers, their spiritual experience of God don't need to be contextualized by the Bible to be confirmed as a God-sighting. If they believe it, that is enough for them. So when Christians approach the subject of studying the Bible it should be to help seekers *better* understand their experience rather than to determine its reliability.

Not only has the ranking of these sources of authority been challenged but the church has been losing its society-based authority the past fifty years. Sexual abuse scandals, a growing mistrust toward authority figures, clergy included, and an overall devaluation of anything wreaking of religious establishment, have contributed to a societal perception that the church has nothing significant to contribute to the spiritual experiences of people.[13] "The church says so" or "the Bible says so" or "Jesus says so" no longer hold the same power to persuade as they did in 1955. Today, people

---

12. Depending on the denomination, this can be true for those who are Christian as well.

13. Pastors complain that their vocational status has been devalued by the public in the past fifty years but I hear the same thing from my physician and attorney friends. We no longer accept a doctor's diagnosis without getting a second opinion or an attorney's promise to get us what we think we deserve. Large companies function with a team model, leveling the playing field to encourage employees to cooperate toward a shared vision. When once we trusted what an authority figure had to say on a particular subject, we now question their view by running an internet search.

have developed their own criteria for authority and use critical thinking to weed out what makes sense to them from what does not. Instead of accepting creeds as a kind of jumping-through-the-hoops exercise to become a Christian, people today want to study those creeds to help them make sense of their spiritual experiences. If they do, then they can accept that method as "authoritative."

To convert seekers to Christianity, Christians demonstrate the usefulness of these other three sources to the formation of their own faith (rather than making the argument one should believe something because the church professes it as the truth). If the other three sources of authority, scripture, reason ("making sense"), and tradition give them a framework to interpret these experiences then they will gain traction (and reason is also gaining value). The other three sources of authority are not meant to discredit our experiences of God outside of the church but rather to help us connect the dots and gain insight into those experiences so that they become life-changing moments. When one has a spiritual experience and then comes to church and finds these other three sources are helpful in faith formation, one will take the first step in answering the question, "What difference does being a Christian make in my life?"

What makes us Christian is that we adhere to the authority of the Bible to inform what we believe (especially our core beliefs) and how we should act, interface with, and intervene in the world. The Bible preserves our history as Israelites (the Old Testament) as well as the history with those who converted to Christianity and became followers of Christ in the New Testament. The teaching of Jesus is our guide for understanding spiritual experiences. If we do not use the Bible as our guide, we might as well let seekers convert us to spiritual seeking (and their experiences can broaden our view of God). The emerging church is embracing the tenets of the Protestant Reformation and reclaiming our freedom to study the Bible and interpret it to be relevant for the faith formation of all generations.

Too often, members insist the pastor offer Bible study but they don't make much effort to show up. Pastors become frustrated when they prepare and then only a few people attend. In 1955, Bible study was held in the morning on a weekday but this no longer works for the majority of people who are working during the day (except for those who are retired). I used to think it was an issue of time and suggest to pastors that they offer Bible study on a weekday evening, Saturday morning, or Sunday evening. But members still don't attend. The problem may not be convenience of time, but biblical illiteracy among members and their shame that they do not know the Bible very well. They are afraid that attending a Bible study will expose their lack of knowledge.[14] When the pastor says, "OK, everyone turn to the book of Obadiah," panic will set in. Everyone will be thinking as they flip through the pages, "OMG, where in the Bible is the book of Obadiah?"

I also find that few members understand the "big picture" of the Bible (i.e., salvation history). If worship leaders use the lectionary, many of the readings are too long. A member can attend worship every Sunday throughout his or her life and still only hear 60 percent of the Bible (the other 40 percent is not in the lectionary). Further, what they hear is a "snippet" of the biblical story and not how each passage contributes to the overarching story of prophecy and its fulfillment in Jesus Christ. Some churches use one scripture reading (although in a Christian worship service not using a gospel or epistle reading feels like something is missing). Some preachers bounce around the Bible, citing one verse here and there (often taken out of context). Bible study should teach Christians how the entire collection of sacred writings weave together to produce a coherent message. This education can be done in the context of worship.

For the builder/silent generation, church life extended throughout the week, but for later generations with seemingly less time, going to church means showing up for worship on Sunday morning. They are unlikely to attend Bible study during the week. Therefore, if worship does not offer Bible study, Christians will no longer have an opportunity to broaden their knowledge. They will be drawn to the "spiritual but not religious" movement because without the Bible, one might as well make meaning of spiritual experiences on one's own. Members need to be taught how to use the Bible for faith formation; they need something more than a spiritual experience of God in worship. Spiritual experiences do not make us Christian and can just as easily make us adherents of another global religion. Essentially, being a Christian means that one says, "I believe the Bible is the Word of God and my guide for understanding my spiritual experiences."

Therefore, Bible study should be a form of worship during the service. It can be done as its own form and/or be interwoven with the sermon. Those who witness may refer to a biblical passage to make clear what they are talking about. Small groups during worship can also engage in Bible study. Worshippers should be prepared to open their Bibles several times during

---

14. Depending on one's denomination, adult education may not be practiced. Many Christians have not studied the Bible since confirmation class.

the worship service to see the interconnection between its stories, references, and themes. Pastors should be well trained in Hebrew and Greek to shed light on the original meaning of a particular word or phrase. To ensure that everyone is on the same page, pastors should select a translation which honors the original text (versus paraphrased Bibles which may be easier to understand but less accurate in their wording).

Worshippers should be encouraged to bring their Bible with them to church. They should memorize the order of the books of the Bible so that they can move from one to another. Some will prefer to have the Bible downloaded on their iPad, Kindle, or iPhone, while others follow easier with the printed page. Whatever medium worshippers choose (printed book or tech-device), they have a way to make notes, connecting their own spiritual experiences to the text.[15] By having a Bible app on one's iPhone, one always has the Bible with them. One can read the Bible when one finds some extra time to just sit and ponder the workings of the world. Worship might also give homework to read a particular passage during the week and to ponder its meaning to be prepared to come to worship on Sunday and talk about it in the small groups.

Witnessing, small groups, and Bible study are all forms of worship that fulfill the mission of converting seekers to Christianity and equipping Christians to put their faith into practice. When I am asked what I anticipate to be one of the most profound changes in the worship of the emerging church, I talk about these three forms of worship. Just as the Protestant Reformation emphasized the religious need for biblical literacy, five hundred years later, we find ourselves neglecting this practice. Church revitalization depends on reviving it. In the future, Christians will spend more time reading the Bible because they will be better equipped to read it on their own. They will feel more confident giving a witness and sharing their faith in small groups. Transformative worship provides a format to help people make sense of their spiritual experiences and equips them to change their lives.

---

15. A collection of these notes may end up being a wonderful legacy for a grandparent to pass on, sharing thoughts and feelings, insights and challenges with their Christian descendants.

Chapter 7

New Rituals in Old Wineskins
Holy Days, Baptisms, Weddings, and Funerals

ONE OF THE MOST common misperceptions I hear from members is that seekers are not interested in attending worship or events hosted by the church. I point out that seekers still attend worship during the holy days, especially Christmas and Easter, and often request a pastor to officiate at a baptism, wedding, or funeral. (They just don't attend worship every week as an expectation of membership.) Even though they are showing less interest in religious organizations than they did even a decade ago, we should note where and when they continue to seek out the church. Disciples start their ministry to convert seekers at this point of connection. While we can offer invitational events such as concerts and coffee shop book studies, I recommend we engage seekers where they are *already* showing interest: holy days and religious rituals. So what we need to do is tweak the way we offer these services so that seekers also become interested in other aspects of congregational life (e.g., weekly worship and mission projects).

The Holy Days

For Christians, Christmas celebrates the birth of the Messiah: the one who came to save us from sin and grant us an eternal relationship with God who became flesh and dwelled among us. For many spiritual seekers and those who do not practice any particular religion (atheists included), Christmas is a season to be generous and express love toward family and friends through gift-giving, sharing a meal, and partying. For Christians and seekers alike,

Christmas is also about an elderly man in a red suit who comes down the chimney to deliver presents. While the celebrations associated with this myth continue to be quite popular in our culture, Christmas Eve worship attendance has decreased significantly. I hear members say their families now gather on Christmas Eve to begin celebrating (as a reason they cannot come to worship). While I don't admit defeat easily, I think we have lost Christmas as a sacred day to secular culture.

In 1955, Christmas Eve summoned the faithful to worship. Members remember when they had to set up folding metal chairs in the back of the sanctuary for those who should have left their homes earlier if they wanted to sit in the pews. They loved that sacred moment holding a candle and experiencing the miracle of Christmas: when the light of Christ breaks forth through the darkness and we recall the incarnation of God in the world. Members report feeling that the Christmas Eve service is one of the most meaningful experiences of God in Christ throughout the liturgical year. They are disappointed when others do not make the same effort to attend. So how might we accommodate to this cultural shift (from attendance at a Christmas Eve service to family celebrations) in order to meet the needs of spiritual seekers (as well as members)? Is there another time we could offer a religious experience as we celebrate the birth of Christ?

Several years ago, observing the steady decline in Christmas Eve worship attendance at the church I served, I suggested we offer a Christmas Eve Eve service on December 23. Those in our community who had family obligations for Christmas Eve could come to church and have a religious experience on a different silent night. They could still light a candle and sing the traditional, beloved hymns, just one night earlier. To offer an additional worship service does involve more time and effort (especially by the pastor and minister of music), but the service can be planned as the same as the one for the following evening. One year we counted the worshippers at each service and surprisingly, the Christmas Eve Eve service was better attended than Christmas Eve. This is another example of how accommodating to cultural shifts can equip Christians to reach spiritual seekers.

Just as the sacred meaning of Christmas has become secularized, Christians could take the secular holidays and make them more sacred. For instance, on New Year's Eve people go to parties to celebrate the past year and toast the coming one. The church could offer worship at 5 p.m. to reflect upon the past year's global, national, and community events (perhaps with a few video clips), giving thanks to God for that which brought about a peaceful resolution. Worshippers pray for the coming year and consider how they may participate in the answers to those prayers. Leaders invite community leaders who made a difference, such as teenagers who worked on a special project to help others or served at the community meal. They could give a witness about how this experience changed their lives. Giving thanks to God and showing appreciation to those who made a difference in the community is a great way to transition from one year to the next.

On New Year's Day (not too early!), the church could offer a service to help worshippers make a resolution and increase their chances of maintaining it over the coming year. Providing space for self-reflection, worshippers decide what to change about themselves and their lives. Worship leaders should use this window of opportunity to announce to seekers what the church offers for support and self-help. During the service, worshippers wrap their resolution (with leftover Christmas paper) to present on the chancel or write it on a postcard. The church then mails the postcard back to them in a few weeks as a reminder of the promises made in the presence of God (along with a reminder of the programs available to change their lives). The pastor preaches a sermon about endurance, patience, and tenacity. Some who fulfilled their resolutions the following year may give a witness to the support they received by being involved in this particular congregation.

In small groups during worship, worshippers may be linked with prayer partners as sources of support to change their lives. They give one another strength to overcome the negativity that threatens to undo one's best intentions. We all know how difficult it is to make a major change about ourselves and people are more likely to succeed if they have someone who can help them navigate over the obstacles and resist temptations. Worship leaders guide discussions for small groups so that partners examine root causes of a particular issue to be resolved such as why one became overweight or is drinking too much. It is important to help people gain insight into their behavior and look toward new behaviors that will bring them a greater sense of satisfaction with life and their relationships. Worship is geared toward helping worshippers envision their lives differently by the end of the year. A service of celebration for those who kept their resolutions and reached their personal goals is another way to reach these people.

Valentine's Day is also a holiday that people like to celebrate but has no religious ritual associated with it. Hallmark, floral shops, and restaurants all provide opportunities for couples to express their love for each other. Couples look for venues to experience a special moment in their relationship, to renew their commitment, to say they are sorry for hurtful things they said and did, and to grow emotionally closer. The sanctuary can be decorated with roses and hearts. Each couple receives a gift from the church. After a sermon about how to argue fairly and have difficult conversations, couples stand in the aisle (while playing a collection of love songs) waiting to approach the chancel and read their renewal of vows to each other, exchange rings and/or receive a blessing. By offering this worship service on February 14 or the day closest to the weekend, the church creates a religious ritual for a secular holiday.

Memorial Day, July 4, and Labor Day are also occasions for the church to provide a worship service for the community. On Memorial Day, the congregation invites friends, family, and neighbors who have experienced a loss over the past year. They are invited forward to sign the memorial book and to write a message to their loved one. The service is geared toward helping people grieve and identifies how being a Christian makes a difference (e.g., we grieve with confidence in eternal life). A service outside is fitting for July 4 and may include a picnic before, after, or during, and celebrates the freedom to express our religious views in a culture of choice. Labor Day is a time to honor those who provide a service to the community, such as the school teachers and other personnel (just as school is getting back after the summer vacation), and to pray for the children and/or do a blessing of the backpacks.

One of my favorite holidays is Thanksgiving. Some churches gather with other churches, to hold a Thanksgiving Eve service. But many people are too busy preparing to host a huge meal the next day, and like Christmas Eve, churches report fewer worshippers in attendance. I suggest offering a Thanksgiving service some time other than the eve of the holiday (and not the weekend after when people begin their Christmas shopping). During this service, worshippers identify all that they are thankful for. They might write their blessings on a paper leaf which is then hung on a tree which is up on the chancel. These blessings are a presentation to and expression of gratefulness to God in Christ. After worshippers come forward and hang their leaves, the tree takes on color and shape. Using different color leaves represents the diversity and abundance of blessing. If possible, after the service, the tree could be placed on the front lawn for the community to see.

New Rituals in Old Wineskins

Baptism and Blessing

During the daytime on Christmas Eve several years ago, a young couple appeared at my office door asking to have their child baptized. They were afraid I was unwilling because the pastor down the street had said "no," because they were not members of a church.[1] I brought them up to the sanctuary and baptized the child and they thanked me and left. Only afterwards did I wonder. Wouldn't it be like God to appear this way? Even though I could imagine some of the church leaders reminding me that baptism should be performed during worship as a ritual of welcoming a baby into a community of believers, something inside me did not want to be the innkeeper who said there is no room for exceptions. Sometimes pastors are called upon to do what they believe is the right thing at the right time.

The theological debate can be summarized as follows: do we require that a parent seeking baptism for their child be church-affiliated or do we accommodate their request to bless the child with the hope they will return on a following Sunday for worship? Those of us who have been officiating baptisms for children and confirmation for teenagers are feeling frustrated because neither approach seems to be achieving the desired result of inspiring parents to bring their children to worship and Christian education. Pastors seek to remain faithful to the theology of baptism, which includes a promise that this particular congregation will be nurturing this particular child's faith. And yet, to insist parents feel obligated to attend church in exchange for baptizing their child is not getting them to attend worship in a culture of choice.

To accommodate the religious needs of seekers, some churches are offering a blessing rather than a baptism for those parents who want God to acknowledge their child but who do not intend to raise their child in the church (and do not want to promise such in the presence of God). This blessing can be performed as a ritual similar to baptism (e.g., asking for support from sponsors/godparents), but without the same level of commitment to and from the congregation. What we don't want to do is twist parents' arms to promise to show up every Sunday for worship, when they know in their hearts they are not going to do so. We don't want to promote the church as a place where one makes promises one does not intend to keep (and one should go home and feel guilty). By offering a different kind

---

1. Some pastors think that this is the way to get people to become members, but I would question if this brings about the desired result.

of ritual such as a blessing, we are meeting the religious needs of seekers and honoring our Christian theology and values.

I've seen pastors create meaningful rituals around the blessing of a child. One pastor invited the entire extended family to the chancel and asked them about their hopes and dreams for the baby's life. The family made promises concerning the care, nurturance, and safety of the child rather than his or her religious upbringing.[2] Prayers focus on the parents' character and nurturing skills, such as compassion, understanding, and empathy. They want the best for their child and this is an opportunity to pray for them to access their inner strength. Unlike a baptism, the congregation does not make promises to a parent who has not yet made the commitment to raise their child in the life of a church.[3] A blessing offers an alternative to a baptism and respects others who have made that commitment. When seekers view the church as a place that tries to be sensitive to their religious needs, they may become interested in having their child baptized at a later date.

For those parents who are ready to make the commitment to bring their child to church every week for worship and education, they can be brought together for baptism classes. Couples who are pregnant search for opportunities to plan for the birth of their child. They look forward to going to see the baby on an ultrasound monitor and hear the baby's heartbeat. They get excited about doing anything baby related. They may look forward to baptism classes to raise their child in the Christian faith. I suggest that one of the pastors teach this class and extend a public invitation to all pregnant couples in the community (and they could still opt for a blessing when the time comes). They receive support from other couples and learn what is involved in raising their child as a Christian.[4] After concluding classes, parents who choose baptism for their child will be well aware of what is involved and the commitment they are making before God.

---

2. Some parents told me that they are not going to bring their child to church because when he or she turns eighteen they can decide for themselves. My response to this is, "Then you have already chosen for them."

3. It's not fair to continue to ask a congregation to read a promise that they will participate in the Christian upbringing of a child (baptism) when everyone is aware that they are unlikely to have the opportunity to do so (for whatever reason, such as that the parents don't live in the area of the church). When parents come to baptize their child and then are not seen again, this reduces a congregation's energy.

4. And what difference raising a child in the Christian faith makes in the life of a family.

New Rituals in Old Wineskins

Weddings

In 1955, most couples were married by an ordained clergyperson who performed a religious ceremony in a religious building. Today, couples are opting to be married in the gazebo at the reception venue, on the beach (and talking over the waves is a challenge!) or in a backyard. Outside of the church, a couple can be married by a justice of the peace or anyone who is authorized by paying a fee on the internet. With more couples choosing one of these nonreligious options, there will be fewer opportunities for pastors to interact with spiritual seekers and introduce them to Christianity. For those who did not grow up in a church, meeting with a pastor to discuss their wedding ceremony may be their first contact with a clergyperson. Some may only be holding their wedding in a church to please their grandmother. And like baptism, some congregations have policies reserving these religious services for those who are members (or related to members).

I used to offer a small group for couples getting married called "wedding seminar." On the first Sunday of the month, every couple who was planning to be married at the church in the coming year was expected to attend worship, immediately followed by wedding seminar. Each month we had a particular topic for conversation (e.g., how to support one another in a time of crisis, what to do when they feel they are drifting apart, how to resolve disagreements, etc.). They developed a behavioral covenant for how to handle situations when they are bringing out the worst in each other (and it's a lot easier to develop a plan when things are going smoothly). They agree on who will do which household tasks and the extent of interference allowed from well-meaning family members. We played games such as "The Newlywed Game" and role played healthy patterns of relating.[5] I assigned homework such as purchasing and putting together a piece of furniture from IKEA (which is quite a test of how well they work together!).

Couples enjoyed coming to wedding seminar and formed relationships with other couples. By the time they were having their ceremony, they were inviting each other to their weddings. When they began talking about attending a church together, it only made sense for them to attend the church that had offered the seminar. What had begun as a time-saver

---

5. This was a television show in the 1960s. They would separate wives and husbands and ask them questions about each other and bring them back together to see if they could guess how the other would answer. If they guessed correctly, they received points to win a prize.

for the pastor (I usually had at least eight couples in wedding seminar per year), became a great way to numerically grow the congregation. Had I used the traditional method of meeting with each couple separately, they likely would have had the wedding ceremony and I would never see them again. These small groups not only provide a setting for pre-marital group counseling but so much more. Several of these couples continue friendships to this day. And by the way, they all joined the church together.

Bridal expositions, often held in convention centers or large halls, have become a popular venue for couples to make wedding preparations. They can meet those who provide services such as music DJs, photographers, decorators, and florists. The venue encompasses a wide range of available choices for their wedding ceremony and reception. Churches can pay a fee for a booth and the pastor and minister of music staff the booth to meet the couples. The table might have pictures of the outside and inside of the church, information about what the wedding service would be like (e.g., samples of vows), and a brochure with fees, expectations, whether the pastor will perform weddings outside of the church, as well as an introduction to the church and its mission to the community. The minister of music may bring a keyboard so that if a couple has a particular song in mind to walk down the aisle to and can hum it, they can hear it played. This is an opportunity for the church staff to interact with spiritual seekers at an important time in their lives.

Funerals

Like weddings and baptisms, spiritual seekers are still requesting clergy to officiate at a funeral or memorial service for their loved one. Some may have met a pastor at a function (such as a wedding reception) or through a friend. They may fondly remember a previous pastor of the church where they grew up as a child. But many seekers have no idea who they would want to officiate at a family member's funeral. They often do not think about this until after their loved one dies. Funeral directors are increasingly aware that their clients are less churched than in days gone by and now keep a list of pastors to call when a spiritual seeker asks "to get somebody."[6] In

---

6. Our rituals for burying the dead are changing. Some services are still held in a church and others at a funeral home (even for long-term members of a congregation). As our church buildings are being sold or repurposed due to the decline in members and finances, funeral homes are buying them. If this trend continues, churches will become

their time of grief, seekers still want religion to help them with their sorrow. Here is another opportunity for pastors to interact with seekers in their time of religious need.

Meanwhile, more pastors are becoming bi-vocational and only work part time at the church. It is more difficult for them to have the time to be the one "got." Pastors put a lot of effort into preparing for funerals; meeting with the family to provide comfort and hear their stories about the life of the one who died. Getting to know someone at the time of their death is not easy and pastors want to get it "right" so that following the funeral the family will say, "It's as if you knew Aunt Betty." Even though pastors may feel they do not have enough time and energy to devote to funerals for those who are not members of the church, this is yet another way to interact with seekers and spark their interest in organized religion. The grieving process is a time when spiritual seekers wonder about the questions of life, death, and the afterlife. "Is it all true?" Tension may arise when members expect that their pastor should be taking care of them rather than those in the community (especially when pastors are part time).

Some churches provide grief ministries to the wider community by commissioning lay ministers who are then assigned to a family member grieving the loss of a loved one. These ministers check in with the family following the funeral and maintain an ongoing relationship through the grieving process. As a pastor officiating at funerals for the loved ones of seekers, I would ask the family if they would like to have someone trained in grief counseling to minister with them in the coming weeks and months.[7] This was a great way to link someone from the church (a Christian) with a spiritual seeker to develop a relationship. Initially, the pastor has to invest some energy and time in training the grief counselors, but this is effort well spent to equip the disciples to do the ministry of Jesus Christ.

I also suggest offering small groups for those who have recently experienced a loss. These groups can be loss-specific (e.g., the death of a family member or a pet, the loss of a job or a significant relationship). Grieving is a process which tends to revive losses from the past. The accumulation of these losses can feel overwhelming. If the congregation is looking for a place to start a ministry to the community and doesn't have the resources for multiple groups, then offer one group for those mourning a significant loss. If the congregation has a social worker who is a member and is willing

---

funeral homes.

7. We used the Stephen Ministries program to equip members for this ministry.

to dedicate their skill to facilitate this group that is a gift, but if not, the pastor can train leaders to serve as facilitators (and there should be something "religious" about these groups). Small groups help seekers to both give and receive comfort from others and talk about their faith. Often, an experience of loss is a time to reflect upon what one really believes.

Just as the trend is toward more personal worship on Sunday morning, baptisms, wedding, and funerals will likely become more personal as well. Because seekers are still seeking out religion for these rituals, it's important that these services are meaningful and meet their religious needs. In 1955, even if someone did not understand what was being said as long as it "sounded" religious, the words were comforting during a funeral. Today, worshippers want to understand what is being said in their effort to make sense of their religious questions. Spiritual seekers are not looking for grand theological jargon to feel close to God but relevant, down-to-earth, everyday language that is easy to understand. Like any experience, especially worship, when one does not know what is going on or what is being said, one tends to tune it out.

If funeral services lose their meaning, seekers will look elsewhere to have their religious needs met following a loss. Because they are seeking something authentic, they are looking for a worship leader who will provide an opportunity for emotional expression. Rout liturgical readings and long scriptural passages can be used as long as they are combined with personal stories, laughter, and tears, and music that stirs the soul. Someone from the congregation may step forward and witness to the work of Christ. If leaders do not provide this experience, seekers will no longer request a pastor to lead a funeral for fear that what they need (e.g., to express sadness) will be suppressed in the service of reading the proper litany. Some families are opting to gather together for a barbecue and tell stories about the departed, remember the good times, lament the bad, look at pictures and videos, cry and hug. They need the emotional (to express feeling) and the cognitive (to make sense of death). A worship service that can interweave both will meet their religious needs.

We want spiritual seekers to show interest in us (and attending worship is a sign of interest), but we often don't have much interest in them. Funerals, weddings, and baptisms are points of contact in which they are still reaching out to the church. Congregations that equip disciples to reach seekers are the ones numerically growing. To practice their faith, disciples may attend a wedding or a funeral, *even if they do not know the family*

New Rituals in Old Wineskins

(and these are public ceremonies). When someone from the church takes the time to be present, especially at a funeral, most seekers appreciate the gesture. A disciples may say, "On behalf of the church we would like to express our sympathy to you for your loss" (or some less formal version). I often hear seekers talk about what it meant to them that someone from the congregation came to their loved one's funeral. This inspires seekers to attend worship just to see what changes people's lives to become so kind and compassionate.

Chapter 8

Music and the Diversity of Religious Needs

Why is music so important to worship?
How does music help the worshipper to access and express feeling?
How does a variety of music help members realize there are a diversity of musical preferences?
How does blended worship serve our mission to convert seekers to Christianity and equip disciples?

I WRITE EVERY MORNING from 6 to 7 o'clock while listening to a classic rock radio station. I like hearing the news, weather, and announcements about which bands are coming to the city that I might want to get tickets to go see. When I finish writing, I go to the gym and get on the treadmill and listen to music on my iPod. After a shower, I get into my car, turn on the radio, and drive to the conference office. When I arrive I put a CD of classical music into the computer while I answer e-mails. I listen to music most of the day (different genres for different settings), only to shift to television watching in the evening (and today many of the shows involve listening to music). Why is music such an essential part of our daily lives? What is its function in worship? How does music help transform the worshipper? What purpose does it serve to convert seekers to Christianity and assist Christians to put their beliefs into practice?

When members identify what is most important to them about the way they worship, they will often talk about the music. They enjoy listening to the voice and handbell choirs and the praise, and the rock and alternative punk instrumental groups. They do so because music is an *emotional connector* to deeply cherished rituals, traditions, events, and people. Whenever the congregation sings "O Little Town of Bethlehem" at Christmas time, I can remember being in church with my family as a young girl and feeling excited about Christmas. At each of my five installations, I have requested a pianist play "Moonlight Sonata" because I remember my mother playing this piece as the prelude to worship. (My mother was the organist at my church growing up.) Christmas Eve would not be Christmas Eve if we didn't sing "Silent Night" while holding candles in the darkness. Music connects us to our feelings and memories of the past.

Through listening to music, singing, and dancing we get in touch with our feelings. In conventional worship, emotion often gets suppressed in favor of rational thought. Through music, worshippers allow these feelings to come to the surface. This is why so many people begin to cry at a funeral or wedding when a favorite piece of music is played. In our society, there are few outlets for uncensored emotion, especially in a collective setting. Because of this lack of opportunity, people long for an emotional experience, even though they may be afraid of feeling conspicuous or ashamed. We tend to isolate ourselves when we need to express an emotion (such as sadness or anger), and yet doing so with others can be reassuring; to know we are not alone. Worship that provides an outlet to laugh and cry, to express anger and joy, to think and feel, meets the religious needs of seekers.

Once we know how we feel, we are able to imagine how someone else feels. So many people in our society struggle with developing empathy and managing their narcissistic tendencies. They look for places to be in touch with and express their feelings. After an experience of "walking a mile in someone else's shoes," they are inspired for social justice. Those who are unaware of how they feel about a crisis or trauma in their past are often unable to to provide empathy and comfort for another. Furthermore, when we can access our own feelings, we are in control over them (and when we cannot access our feelings, they can take control over us). Healthy relationships depend on being able to access and manage one's feelings so one can acknowledge the feelings of others. In addition to small-group sharing, music is another avenue for emotional expression.

Traditional worship, especially in the mainline church, has emphasized the rational through forms of worship such as sermons and readings that ask the worshipper to make sense of what is being said. The transformative nature of worship is geared toward helping people to think differently so that they will come to believe or strengthen their belief in Christ. Christian education, likewise, serves to teach children how to read and understand the Bible so they will grow in wisdom and stature and in favor with God. The builder/silent generation responds well to worship as an exercise in thinking (and they do not tend to express emotion in the presence of others). For them, a good sermon should be "food for thought" throughout the week. In 1955, one became a Christian as a child through education (Sunday school and confirmation class). One learned how to think like a Christian.

Younger generations tend to be more comfortable expressing emotion. Intimacy of thought (personal sharing) combined with expressing emotion, helps them to feel more connected to others and God in Christ. They want a religious experience that encourages worshippers to be genuine and authentic. They have enough places in their lives where they have to conceal how they are feeling, push back tears, and swallow anger and frustration. They long for places to share what is really going on in their lives, express how they feel about events, and discern where God intervenes. They find strength from others when God seems to be missing. They yearn for a sense of emotional connectedness to others, helping them to feel less isolated and alone in the world. In a culture where so many work at a cubicle or from home on the internet, the church may emerge as the one place in our society where people gather in-person for meaningful face-to-face interaction.

The internet has increased levels of interaction between and among people via blogging, tweeting, posting, Skype, GoToMeeting, Google chat, etc. Social media provides a forum for individuals to communicate, share thoughts and experiences, and even to express emotion. Internet worship will likely continue to gain traction. But I think there is no substitute for expressing sadness, grief, disappointment, and joy, love, and compassion in the actual company of others who understand how one feels. For some, the church is one of the few places where they can relate to others in a non-technological environment (and this may explain why coffee shops and bars are hang-out places to play board games and talk). The church, therefore, should create space for people to share what is going on in their lives and play music that speaks to their heart so they can access their feelings.

To plan a worship service that meets the religious needs of Christians and seekers alike, the worship team (comprised of at least one from each generation) comes together to listen to a variety of music genres, from classical to punk, hip-hop, rap, classic and contemporary rock, and country.

Then, ask each other, "How do you feel as you listen to this piece of music? Does it make you feel more spiritually connected to God in Christ? Worship planning takes emotions into consideration (and sometimes the team may want to identify one emotion to create a mood throughout the worship experience). For instance, if the purpose of a worship service is to help worshippers to mourn, the team may select music that prompts them to feel sad (versus a bouncy beat that makes them feel like getting up to dance after they have mourned). If the purpose is to provoke anger for an injustice, the team looks for music that instigates people for action. Music can generate a feeling to motivate Christians to put their beliefs into practice.

Balancing the Diversity of Musical Needs among All Worshippers

In a culture of obligation, when everyone had to attend worship, it didn't matter who liked what kind of music. During the shift to a culture of choice, members began to think about which genres of music they like hearing in worship (e.g., classical music). Interestingly, when the levee broke and they realized not only they had a choice, but others did as well, they clung to the traditional music they were used to hearing on Sunday morning. Some describe traditional music as "sacred" and declared all other music offensive to God.[1] Because of their long-term affiliation with the church, some members insist that their religious needs be met above and beyond everyone else's (seekers and other members). For those who like traditional music, they tend to have little tolerance for drums, keyboards, and guitars. Seemingly perplexed, they cannot understand why others do not want to worship the same way they do.

Pastors often enable the preferential treatment of a few members in exchange for volunteerism. As the number of members shrinks, the need for more hands to do the same amount of work increases. Pastors get hooked by this dynamic when they attempt to please these members because, without them, things might not get done around the church. Fear and anxiety loom large. The more these members complain about nontraditional music, the more the pastor focuses on their religious needs even if it means sacrificing the needs of others. In response, leaders plan a worship service to sing the favorite hymns of the current membership. To do so appears to be in the best interests of the church. But when the pastor and

---

1. Who gets to decide what is defined as sacred music?

other leaders cater to a select few at the expense of many, others will feel their religious needs are being cast aside. They may become inactive or seek out a worshipping community that offers a wider selection of music to meet a wider range of worshippers' preferences.

Contemporary worship was an attempt to acknowledge that not everyone is looking for worship as the singing of traditional hymns. In many churches, the major difference between traditional and contemporary worship is the musical genres. Whereas traditional worship is designed to sing three hymns out of the same hymnal, sung collectively to the accompaniment of an organist, contemporary music tends to be more upbeat, rhythmic and lyrically repetitive. Congregations form praise bands comprised of members from the younger generations. Those who are hungry to hear something different, who want more energy and participation in the worship experience, like the change in music. Those who perceive the pipe organ to be God's favorite instrument, are annoyed. Had there been less resistance to change in general, many churches might have been able to recognize that individual worshippers have diverse religious needs. It isn't contemporary worship that held any promise to save the day, it is members' willingness to let go of some of their own needs to meet the needs of others.

The contemporary versus traditional worship debate addresses the question: should leaders attempt to meet the diversity of religious needs in the same worship service or offer multiple worship services each one geared toward one generation? Some churches answer this question by holding two worship services: one traditional and one contemporary. Those who prefer traditional music attend traditional worship and those who prefer contemporary music attend contemporary worship. Reflecting back on this shift, I think now that contemporary worship was viewed as a quick fix to meet the religious needs of those whose needs were not being met with traditional music. This approach solves the immediate problem for those who prefer one style of music over another, but it doesn't help worshippers to experience a diverse range of music in the pursuit of faith formation and emotional expression. Introducing new music is an opportunity to adapt to change. One might even be surprised to have a spiritual experience with a different kind of music.

Over the last several years, with the church's focus on one genre of music, contemporary worship is suffering the same fate as traditional worship by narrowing on the religious needs of one generation (or a particular group of members). As the numbers dwindle for contemporary worship, there has been a regressive pull back toward traditional worship (as defined by music). Few churches still offer contemporary worship. Those who couldn't make the transition back either stayed home or went elsewhere. As a result, the church has fewer dollars to pay pastors full time, and so in the interest of time, many churches reverted to one worship service again. This wasn't the worst thing that could have happened. What arose was a new style referred to as "blended worship," a combination of both traditional and contemporary music.[2] Blended worship embodies a host of worship preferences and is an adaptive challenge to meeting the religious needs of diverse people with respect to age, race, and ethnicity.

Unlike traditional and contemporary, blended worship raises the awareness of members by observing others responding to music by dancing, singing, and clapping. When they see another generation enjoying a song they may not like, their hearts may soften so that they will no longer insist worship meet their religious needs 100 percent of the time. Watching teens in a balcony singing music familiar to them and excited to be in worship should inspire members to set aside some of their own needs. Members transitioning to become disciples are willing to forgo some of their own religious needs to meet the religious needs of others (even if they do not like the music!). Such sacrifice is what Jesus calls us to do. To become a disciple, members recognize their need to convert seekers is stronger than their need to sing from one genre of music. And we are not just talking about music here, but it's a good place to start when it comes to equipping members to put their faith into practice.

Worship is not intended to be "all about me" and my needs nor a gathering of demographically related people who share a similar worldview, social location, and ideology (as if this is the basis for developing a shared theological outlook).[3] Even though we can assess satisfaction levels to ensure that some needs are being met, our quest is to move people away from the premise that worship should meet their religious needs 100 percent of the time.[4] This approach to worship sustains an inward focus instead of an

---

2. An example is when the congregation sings a praise song and then on the last note, begins to sing a traditional hymn (e.g., worshippers sing "Shine, Jesus, Shine" and then immediately sing "Rock of Ages."

3. Last I checked, worship was directed to God in Christ and not individual worshippers.

4. If worship is meant to meet each individual's religious needs 100 percent of the time (a goal which I do not perceive to be realistic or faithful), then we need to offer as many worship services as there are genres of music (e.g., one for those who like classical,

outward focus. Transformative worship is an exercise in adaptability and flexibility toward change in order to meet the religious needs of others. Those congregations called to discipleship will let go of some of their own needs to meet the needs of others.

Here, we may note that not every individual within every demographic likes the same kind of music. Every individual has his or her own music preferences. While each of us is born into or chooses to associate with our cultural groupings, we are a combination of cultural variables and multiple affiliations. Further, each of us has different levels of strength in our emotional connection with these variables and affiliations. And yet, as I have observed throughout this book, we can generalize about the preferences of particular generations. But, we should be mindful that each individual is unique. Even though the majority in a certain age range may like certain kinds of music, others may like the music of other generations. In numerically growing congregations, it is more important to have a diverse group of people with whom to worship, than to worship exclusively with those who share their preference for music.

Pastors and leaders should figure worship can meet the religious needs of the individual somewhere between 40 and 60 percent of the time. What is becoming clear is that we cannot continue to sing the same three traditional hymns and convert seekers to Christianity. They are probably unfamiliar with hymns and may not like this genre (perhaps preferring something more upbeat such as praise music). When "Rock of Ages" is sung three times in the same worship service (and singing three hymns out of the same hymnal sounds like singing the same hymn three times when you don't know the hymns), it creates a perception that those who are already Christian are the ones whose religious needs will be met. We cannot continue to do things the same way and expect seekers to become Christian. We cannot try to change others (i.e., convince seekers that they should want to sing these hymns). Instead, we want to demonstrate that

---

one for those who like rap, etc.). But because music does tend to be generationally linked, we may end up with a worship service filled with worshippers of a specific age. While everyone may like the music, something else will be missing (and if you don't know what this "something" is, ask someone who attends a mainline church where everyone is over the age of seventy). Leaders who take this approach enable segregation to continue in the mainline church. Racial/ethnic and generational diversity can only be achieved when we are willing to listen to a variety of music. I would rather worship with a diversity of worshippers than worry about whether I like the music played during the worship service.

what it means to be a Christian is to be willing to change. If this means singing music in worship that is "not my cup of tea," then so be it.

When the pastor encounters a high level of resistance to new music in the worship service (e.g., "if you continue to play that kind of music, I will leave the church"), then he or she is being held hostage from making needed changes. In some churches, this will be the end of the discussion and the pastor will resign to the fact that he or she has just been designated the chaplain of a dying organization. When resistance is highly charged, it may not be worth the pastor's energy. That energy may be better used to start a second service (or a new church) as long as the members are willing to support the pastor's efforts financially, emotionally, and spiritually (e.g., they will invite friends, family, and neighbors to attend the second service). The pastor should also be given creative license and liturgical freedom to design and experiment with new forms of worship including other instruments and/or prerecorded music. A second service can open a window of fresh air for a pastor who has felt suffocated by the expectations of members to meet their needs exclusively.

Instrumentals and a Variety of Music

Glorifying God and making a joyful noise can be done with a variety of different instruments as long as those playing them and those listening are experiencing the joy of worship. For the builder/silent generation, organ music is associated with "being in church" in the presence of God in Christ. They want an organist to play the organ and preferably be trained in classical music. But today, fewer young people are learning to play the organ and therefore finding an organist is becoming difficult. Perhaps because of this trend, current organists are continuing to play well into their elder years. These organists perceive they are helping the church and members are quite appreciative. But if the congregation's preferences for music are shifting to more contemporary genres, they don't want to hurt the feelings of the current organist by suggesting retirement. So nothing changes. When they all do retire, it is unlikely that the organ will continue as the sole instrument associated with music in worship.[5]

---

5. The issue for congregations will be whether to repair an organ when it breaks, especially if to do so is expensive. Couples getting married may still request organ music for the processional and recessional, and families may still request organ music for a funeral. It's a tough call.

For those churches already making this transition, they are not hiring another organist but a minister of music who functions more as a "coordinator" of the music ministry in the church. He or she does not necessarily play the instruments (although should have musical abilities). The minister of music assists the congregation to fulfill their mission of converting seekers and equipping disciples (hence, the title "minister"). He or she develops relationships with worshippers to identify who plays an instrument or sings, even if they haven't played for a while and may give lessons to those who are willing to learn (in exchange for playing their instrument or singing in a worship service). There are likely people in the community who would be interested in playing in an orchestra or band who would not find their way into a church otherwise. For children who do not play an instrument and do not want to sing, teaching them how to play the recorder is a great way to include them in worship.

Traditionally, prerecorded music has been viewed as taboo, yet today, its use is becoming more acceptable in worship. This is largely due to the technological advances in sound systems. (The boom-box days are over.) Churches are updating their sound systems to a superior quality allowing for iPods and CDs to be played. A decent sound system (and there is nothing worse than a bad sound system in worship) affords worshippers the opportunity to bring their own music (and encourages teenagers to do so) to be played during worship. Contemporary pop and rap musicians sing about Jesus, God, religion, and compassion. We have access to a reservoir of music. For seekers who are unfamiliar with other forms of worship, hearing familiar music can make them feel more comfortable. For Christians who are desperately seeking more contemporary music, they can play whatever appeals to them. Investing in a good sound system is a good use of limited resources for a church that wants to reach out and attract new people.

Another change happening in the emerging church is that worshippers are no longer reading the lyrics on a screen or out of a hymnal. When worshippers bring their own music, it is likely others will know the lyrics and be able to sing along. I also suggest congregations memorize songs. They can practice singing these songs in the car, at a party, or in the shower.[6] Visitors can download lyrics they do not know beforehand. They may also just pick up some of the words and try to sing along, especially if the music generates energy and enthusiasm. When worshippers know the music and

---

6. Honestly, I am amazed when long-term members still need a hymnal to sing a beloved song they have sung a hundred times.

can sing along, worship has a different feel than when everyone's eyes are glued to the printed word. Singing music without a hymnal in one's hand affords the worshipper the freedom to move about and dance and make eye contact with other worshippers. It increases the level of intimacy between and among worshippers.

Forms of Meditation: Stillness and Silence

We live in a fast-paced, multitasking society. Most of us don't sit still long enough to feel anything. We fill our days with errands, agendas, and constant movement so that by the end of the day we are exhausted. All we can manage to do is sit in front of the television and zone out. Our culture places tremendous value on productivity translated into "getting things done to feel as if our lives have purpose." Sitting still confronts us with how we are feeling (e.g., sadness, depression, or anger). We move hastily to be one step ahead of these feelings (activity can suppress feelings). This makes the setting of worship (sitting passively in a pew) unappealing for those who are trying to escape from their feelings. Within a supportive environment, however, stillness can be an opportunity to change the way we manage and express our feelings.

Most visitors will struggle with sitting still. Members have become accustomed to this posture of worship over the years, but after about an hour (considered the proper amount of time for a worship service in mainline religion), they may appear to squirm a bit, much to the annoyance of the pastor and worship leaders. If worship offers a moment of silence for personal prayer, most leaders allow less than one minute.[7] As long as the worshippers have something to focus on they seem to enjoy worship, but complete silence and stillness is so counter-cultural that it is likely to raise anxiety. Silence, therefore, should be introduced or expanded in short intervals so as to give worshippers time to increase their tolerance and appreciate its value.

---

7. Some churches avoid silence and stillness altogether. If silence raises the anxiety of the pastor, he or she is likely to pass over it quickly, a gesture which may make the congregation anxious. Some silence is used as a form of confession and worshippers may associate silence with identifying what they have done wrong, which may conjure up feelings of guilt and shame. Worship is not usually intended to help people deal with feelings; to acknowledge, manage, cope, and appropriately express and let-go so as to know divine forgiveness and make amends. Pastors may need to initially walk through the variety of feelings when we come into the presence of God in Christ so that worshippers feel equipped to handle them.

Transformative Worship

Most worship packs a lot of education into a very short period of time, leaving the worshipper little chance to assimilate, filter, and sort through all the information (therefore, worshippers have trouble recalling what the sermon was about later during the week). We move from one form to another so that worship appears "seamless," but if it moves too fast, worshippers can't catch up, and will fall behind and lose interest.[8] Stillness and silence can also be used at key points when pausing may help the worshipper to reflect upon and ponder what has just been said as well as what God might be trying to say. Giving the worshipper time to reflect upon what is being said allows time for them to connect it to their spiritual experiences. Most worshippers are trying to listen to what the worship leader is saying, but they also need time just to be still and experience God.

Yoga can be used as a form for transformative worship (especially if worship focuses on the liturgical arts). Worshippers are invited to bring their exercise mats with them to worship (and alternative postures should be offered for those who cannot physically get onto the floor). They should dress comfortably to allow for maximum flexibility and mirror the postures assumed by the leader. In each pose, they are invited to listen to the voice of God, with the premise that changing positions can produce a change in perspective (insight). Posturing themselves into prayerful positions, this form of worship integrates the body, mind, and soul, a practice associated with spirituality. Most churches have space in their fellowship halls that can be used for this purpose. I would recommend that something "religious" be done, so that those who attend know they have not just had a yoga class at the local gym, but have attended a church worship service.

Moments of silence also allow the worship team time to worship themselves. Many pastors and worship leaders feel "on" and do not immerse themselves in the religious experience. If there has been a lot of emotion expressed, silence can give them time to express their own feelings and then collect themselves and make changes to the worship service to better reflect the current mood among worshippers. Having been a pastor myself, I can identify with the constant movement (and I, too, felt like I needed to control the flow of worship). We were taught that the entire worship service should be well-planned and well-executed in order to avoid mistakes. Yet, to do so squeezed out the possibility of spontaneity and creativity. We moved from one form of worship to the next, wrote everything down so

---

8. Some worship forms last too long. I recommend a *Sesame Street* style where one form doesn't last more than a few minutes before moving or overlapping to the next form.

as not to lose our place and feel anxious. When we allow ourselves to feel vulnerable in these pauses, we get caught up in the movement of the Holy Spirit and actually experience worship in a new way.

Not all meditation has to be an exercise in silence. Music can be played in the background. Classical music is good for this but I like the sounds of the seascape and forest as well as seasonal music. Worshippers may not be paying attention to the music (they are supposed to be listening to God), but the music helps them to feel God's presence in a way that speaking does not. I would suggest that silence and listening to music be done four times in a worship service, spread out at various moments when reflection is called for (e.g., after the sermon, before or after the prayer, after the commission when the homework is given). Initially, worshippers may find this boring but in time they will find this counter-cultural aspect of worship an opportunity to feel more connected to God. The objective is to teach the worshipper how to practice silence and stillness (as a form of meditation) at other times in their daily lives.

In 1955, silence during worship was less important because the process of converting and applying beliefs entailed the pastor preaching and the people believing it. Today, worshippers need time to think about what is being said and to decide for themselves whether it helps them make sense of their spiritual experiences. Worshippers require silence to embark upon decision-making and clear their thoughts of worries, concerns, and anxieties (by first becoming aware of them). Spiritual meditation can also be done in a more guided form (e.g., a leader offers a journey or image and worshippers freely associate whatever comes to mind). The function of silence is to help the worshipper attach feeling to what they are thinking about; to integrate thoughts and feelings, the rational with the emotional. This process is what helps people to change their lives.

Liturgical Dance, Pilgrimage, and Other Forms of Movement

In the church I most recently served, we had two liturgical dance troupes: one that was more of a practice group for young children who would learn the moves, have fun, and occasionally dance in worship. When they turned around eight years old, they graduated to the liturgical troupe, which dances in worship on a regular basis. Many attended dancing school in the congregation and this was an opportunity to invite their friends to participate. This is a great way to get teenagers involved in worship.

For churches renting out space to a local dancing school, they may have a ready-made dance troupe in their own church building. Ask the dance teacher who he or she would recommend as a liturgical dance teacher (among one of the teenagers), and pay that teenager to be the troupe's leader. He or she is likely to invite others from the dancing school to add dancers to the troupe with those who are already part of the congregation. Or, a church may decide to offer free rent to a dancing school in exchange for dancers on holy days (and most dancing schools are trying to keep costs down, so will jump at this opportunity). I often hear from dancing school teachers who rent space from a church that no one from the congregation has ever asked them to participate in the worship service. They are often pleasantly surprised to learn that dance is becoming an important form of worship. I also hear people say, "Any church that wants teenagers to be dancing in the aisle is the church for me."[9]

Liturgical dance can be done in two forms: pre-form and free-form. Pre-form is when the worshippers watch the liturgical dancers who have rehearsed and are now performing. Free-form is when someone leads the body movements and the worshippers attempt to follow, or it could be without a leader and all worshippers do their own thing. Pre-form requires more effort in that the congregation needs to have a teacher who is assigned the task of providing the instruction (as suggested above) and the troupe is likely to have weekly rehearsals (or more depending on the amount of practice needed). Free-form takes some encouragement so that worshippers move their body (e.g., swing their arms) to the music. I suggest using a combination of both in worship to meet the religious needs of a wider range of people.

---

9. Yes, I have also heard some negative comments. When we first introduced liturgical dance in the worship service, there were many who did not like it. These people became the church's best evangelists, as when they were out in the community, they were asked, "Do you attend that church where the kids are dancing in the aisles?" And they would respond, "Yes, and I thought I would hate it, but I found I love it!"

Chapter 9

The Setting of Transformative Worship
Space, Time, and Imagination

> *Do millennials want to worship in our church building?*
> *Should we remove the pews and replace them with chairs?*
> *What are visitors thinking about when they enter the sanctuary?*
> *What times should we offer worship to attract new people?*

To convert spiritual seekers to Christianity and equip Christians to put their beliefs into practice, the setting of worship should be evaluated: its physical space, curb appeal, the times and days offered, and the configuration of pews/chairs. In this chapter, I will explore the setting and what might need to change for transformative worship.

The Building Dilemma

As a church growth consultant, I am frequently asked about the future of church buildings. Do millennials want to worship in traditional buildings or in store fronts, cafes, and bars? Does the congregation believe that God wants them to reach out to a different mission field than in the past? Has the mission field moved to another location? Should we sell our building and move to a new location in order to reach this mission field? (Admittedly, I'm not asked this question very often.) Is it faithful stewardship to continue to use the endowment to pay for utilities when the congregation has decreased to a few people who have long since left the neighborhood but travel some distance so that they can worship in the church of their childhood?[1] When talking about the building we are faced once again with the great dilemma: do we put aside our own religious needs to provide a religious home for spiritual seekers?[2]

By this point in the book, the reader has realized that in order to convert seekers to Christianity, the church needs members to convert to disciples who are flexible for change, and are willing to adapt to the current challenges and make decisions based on what they believe God wants rather than what they want. Some may be wondering just how accommodating they should become to grow the congregation. Numerical decline is a symptom that members are working really hard to convert others but not themselves. Those congregations turning around their decline are willing to do whatever is necessary to convert seekers to Christianity even if that entails selling their building. I am not suggesting that all a congregation has to do to numerically grow is to change locations but disciples should be more concerned about people than buildings.

The church is a sacred building. Because members have experienced the presence of God in this place, they form an emotional connection with the space itself. With fondness, they recall special events in their lives: walking down the aisle to be married, baptizing their children, and celebrating the lives of family members. Some members have family roots extending for several generations, noted by brass memorial plaques on the pews and dedications on steeples and organs. When they are in the church building, they feel spiritually closer to all those who have gone before; the building functions as a kind of transitional object to connect them with those in heaven. Letting go of the building can be one of the most emotionally difficult decisions a congregation has to make. It is truly a leap of faith.[3]

---

1. A congregation should prayerfully consider if the person who gave this money intended it to be used for this purpose.

2. I have found that many congregations are afraid to answer these questions. In their denial, they default to being dependent upon their remaining funds (e.g., endowment) to take care of the building so that they can worship in their beloved church until the day they die.

3. We want people to have a relationship with the setting of worship but we do not want to enable an attachment disorder that prevents them from making sound decisions. They should experience God in the sanctuary but outside as well. The issue is when the setting takes priority over purpose: members would prefer to continue to worship in a space because of fond memories rather than creating new memories of living out Jesus' commission to convert spiritual seekers to Christianity.

The Setting of Transformative Worship

The building question relates to the church's mission and theological understanding of what God in Christ intends for the future. If the purpose is to convert spiritual seekers to Christianity *and that is no longer happening* in the current location, then the congregation should explore other options. If spiritual seekers are living and/or working in the neighborhood (and this conclusion is based on a demographic report of facts not perception), then the location of the building may not be the problem to be solved. But if seekers have moved to another neighborhood, then selling the building is an option. Simply selling the building and renting or purchasing another is not a quick fix that seekers will come. When a new church arrives in a new neighborhood, they are often distrusted until they establish credibility. A congregation moving into a new neighborhood should engage in community projects to form relationships with their neighbors.

A church building may be in a good location, but cry for cosmetic changes to increase its overall curb appeal (e.g., signage, religious symbols, landscaping, paved parking lot, etc.). Bring together a group who do not attend the church or who have recently visited and ask them the following questions: Does the building appear to be well-cared for? (A well-cared for facility communicates to the community they care about those who come inside.)[4] Is the church easy to find from the main road and if not, how might we improve the access? (I cannot tell you how many times GPS said I had arrived and I couldn't see the church.) Is it well marked which way to come into the parking lot and easy to locate a space to park? (Driving around trying to find a parking space is not a good way for a seeker to begin their experience of church.) Or are there so few cars in the parking lot that visitors wonder if they have the wrong time for worship? Newer churches tend to pave their parking lots in front to emphasize how many people are in worship.

What Are Visitors Thinking About When They Enter the Sanctuary?

Most of our church buildings were architecturally designed so that everyone would come in through the front door. This was done intentionally so that worshippers experience a wow-factor at the entrance to the sanctuary. As they enter, they behold the chancel, the cross, the paintings, and other

---

4. A facility that is not well-cared for may imply members have no money to fix it up and are hoping for new members to increase their income.

Christian symbols that make people feel they are stepping onto sacred ground. Yet, members tend to enter the building via the closest door from the parking lot to the sanctuary. This route may lead visitors through a side door or the front of the sanctuary facing the back. Visitors tend to follow the flow from the parking lot. This way they miss the wow-factor. To practice discipleship, all members (with the exception of those with physical limitations) should enter the building through the front door. Neighbors then see people walking into the church and may become inspired to attend.[5]

In one church where I served as pastor, we conducted a survey asking visitors what they were thinking when they entered the sanctuary. We received some very interesting answers. Themes began to emerge that we found helpful to practice hospitality. For instance, many visitors told us they were combing the pews looking for "like" people (e.g., a thirty-something mother with kids was looking for another thirty-something mother with kids). We also learned that visitors form an impression based on the number of worshippers: are the pews filled with people excited to be in worship or are there a lot of empty pews? Full pews imply that the church offers a religious experience that changes lives, whereas empty pews imply those in attendance feel obligated to be present. The difference communicates whether the leadership is working toward meeting the religious needs of all or just a few. The perception of "full" pews is a predictor of whether a visitor will return the following Sunday.[6]

Some churches are removing their pews (and putting them in storage for the future) and purchasing stackable, comfortable chairs.[7] If the congregation is going to use small groups during worship, then chairs work better in that they can be reconfigured into circles. Chairs can also mimic pews by being placed in rows with a center aisle to accommodate a large crowd (e.g., a wedding) and be easily moved during a worship service. The space should support the forms of worship.[8] The question is not, "how would we offer small groups in pews?" but, "what kind of seating do we need to offer small groups as a form of worship?" I also suggest the purchase of small

---

5. When I consult with congregations I will often knock on the doors of their neighbors and talk with them. When members park in the back of the building, I often hear neighbors wondering if the church is still open as they never see anyone going in there.

6. Alice Mann says this is at 80 percent seating capacity.

7. How many chairs are set up for worship depends on the average attendance in worship.

8. Too often, we approach change the other way around: we can't do small groups during worship because our space does not allow us to do so.

round tables for the worship space. Tables make it more conducive to drink coffee (and perhaps to also serve food) and use one's tech device (what I call "high test-high tech" worship space).

The First Five Minutes

In 1955, we practiced hospitality to visitors by being "warm and friendly" and inviting them downstairs to coffee hour following the worship service. Members expected the pastor to show up at the visitor's home either later that afternoon or on Monday morning. A water bottle with the church's logo or a loaf of bread was given to them as a welcome gift. The premise of hospitality was that as long as a visitor felt welcomed by the members, they would return the following Sunday. But today, visitors are looking for a religious experience that will change their lives by helping them to make sense of their spiritual experiences of God. They are less concerned with feeling welcomed and more concerned about how the church facilitates this process of conversion. Seekers may not need to feel welcomed at all (counter-Walmart philosophy where everyone is greeted as they walk through the door).

It is often presumed that visitors make a decision about whether or not they will return a second Sunday some time during the worship service. Research has attempted to determine just when and based on what factors visitors make this decision. In 1955, it was thought that visitors decided after worship (which was one of the reasons why congregations began serving coffee so they could be introduced to members), but more recently, we realize they decide sooner rather than later. Some say they make their decision in the first ten minutes of worship; yet I think it is more likely in the first five minutes. But visitors don't know they are supposed to wait until the organist starts playing the prelude. They are deciding as they pull into the driveway, get out of the car, and walk into the church. Therefore, variables such as curb appeal, signs directing the way to the sanctuary, updated restrooms, and a welcoming spirit all factor into their decision.

I became aware of the narrow window of opportunity churches have to impress visitors when I moved from Boston to Harrisburg a few years ago. I looked at a number of houses before making my purchase. Initially, the real estate broker scheduled appointments thirty minutes apart, but I knew whether this was "the" house or not in less than five minutes. My first impression weighed 80 percent (in the first few seconds) and as I looked around the house, I formulated the other 20 percent. If my initial impression of the house was positive, then I weighed things which needed to be fixed as minor, but if it was 80 percent negative, those same problems seemed major. Visitors to a worship service also form a first impression, which may actually have nothing to do with the worship service per se and everything to do with the ease with which they walk from their car to the sanctuary and how people respond to them along the way.

What do visitors experience when they open the front door of a church? Is it evident which door to enter or do they have to keep pulling on door handles to figure out which door is open?[9] We do not want visitors to wander through the church, which can feel like being lost in a corn maze as they try to find their way to the restroom, sanctuary, or fellowship hall. Because long-term members know how to find their way around the church building, they assume that everyone else should be able to as well. Signs help as long as they are professionally or artistically crafted and placed in well-lit and easy-to-see locations. Being locked out or not knowing which way to go to reach the sanctuary conveys to visitors that members are not interested in their "lost-ness." This is not how we want visitors to form their first impression of the church.

When visitors enter a sanctuary before the worship service begins, they hear a lot of chatter. Members are hugging each other, talking about their lives, sharing recent events and prayer concerns. From members' perspective, before and after worship is a time of personal interaction that they look forward to throughout the week. But to visitors, all they hear is a buzz of activity. They anticipate worshippers would be preparing to worship God in Christ by reading their Bibles and praying, not discussing committee work or the latest controversy circulating among the congregation.[10] I encourage churches to provide space (with coffee) to allow for conversation outside of the sanctuary (before and after worship) so that if one wants to talk, they have a place to do so. We need to create an etiquette of spiritual preparedness before worship begins in the sanctuary. Playing music (either live or recorded) can facilitate this process.

---

9. Many churches lock their doors as a safe church policy.

10. We want worshippers to talk with each other in the small groups during worship, but the sanctuary should feel like sacred space to visitors and not a social hall.

The Setting of Transformative Worship

The Time of Worship and Offering Multiple Services

When we were still a Christian nation in 1955, everyone went to church on Sunday morning. Most television sets received signals from only three stations.[11] The stores were closed and very few people worked (with the exception of hospital personnel and emergency responders). Sport games and their practices were not held on Sunday. For Christians, Saturday was the day to do errands and Sunday was time set aside for church and family. In a culture of obligation, when the Sabbath was honored and protected by law, Sunday morning was reserved to worship God in Christ. Then the blue laws were repealed and a significant number of people began working on Sunday, allowing another significant number of people to shop, play, and sleep in. Attending worship became one among many options of "what to do" with one's Sunday morning. In a culture of obligation, one service per week was sufficient, but in a multi-optional culture, multiple services are now necessary to provide people with a choice of time.

It is unlikely that Sunday morning will continue to be the hour for worship or at least the only option in the emerging church.[12] Other venues (movie theaters and health clubs) know that they have to offer multiple times in a culture of choice.[13] Numerically growing congregations attempt to meet the needs of their community by expanding the options to make attending worship more convenient. Those who insist the church offer only one worship service at 10 o'clock on Sunday morning will be less likely to attract new people and may lose their own members to churches that offer multiple worship times.[14] Not only is this a good way to attract seekers to worship, but members who work on Sunday will appreciate being able to attend worship at another time. As we shift to a culture of choice, multiple worship services will become more commonplace.

Whenever I suggest that a church begin a second worship service, someone inevitably responds, "But we can't fill the pews for the worship service we have now!" In 1955, the reason to begin a second service was because the first service could no longer accommodate the overflow of

---

11. And there was usually nothing "good" on.

12. Much of the decline in our churches is a result of our maintaining the status quo of one hour on Sunday morning.

13. There is a new trend in health clubs to be open twenty-four hours a day.

14. Some congregations are afraid to offer multiple worship times for fear that the church will become a place of multiple congregations. While I am not sure why that would be problematic, there are ways of encouraging interaction among all those who attend.

bodies in the pews. Late arrivers had to stand in the back of the sanctuary (or sit on metal chairs) when they couldn't find an empty pew. Today, the reason to offer a second or multiple worship services has changed: we are trying to adjust to people's schedules (especially work) so as to make worship accessible. Multiple services communicates to the community that the church cares about them and genuinely wants them to come and worship. It challenges the misperception that Christians only want to attract people who are willing "to do things the way we have always done them."

Emerging churches are experimenting with alternative times and days to discern what works for the spiritual seekers in their neighborhood. When to offer worship services should be based on demographics (i.e., who is in the neighborhood and what they are looking for from a church). If, for instance, the church is surrounded by assisted living facilities and the average age is eighty, then Sunday morning is probably the best time because the builder/silent generation is accustomed to that time and may not want to go out in the evening. If your church is in a downtown area that comes alive at night in the restaurants and bars, a morning worship service is probably *not* the best time to attract the millennial generation. Try experimenting with a 7 p.m. or even 10 p.m. worship time on a Saturday night. This gives them the option to attend worship before going out for the evening.

Other factors I take into consideration is the percentage of Catholics in a given neighborhood. On a demographics report, more than 33 percent of Catholics suggest that there is already a cultural norm of attending worship on Saturday afternoon. The priest of the local Catholic Church can give an estimate of attendance to compare Saturday afternoon to Sunday morning. This is useful information, especially if he says that the Saturday afternoon worship service is better attended than Sunday morning. If this is the case, I recommend a Saturday afternoon worship service. Protestants in a Catholic area are likely familiar with the idea of a Saturday worship service. Even though they may associate the time with being Catholic, in time they will appreciate having the option in a culture of choice.

Consider offering several worship services at different times during the week. If the congregation employs a worship team, start a second team and then each team can rotate between the different services. For a church to numerically grow by converting members to disciples and seekers to Christianity, I recommend offering *three to five worship services throughout the week* (even if the present congregation is numerically small). Be creative with the days and times (and if one time is out of sync with the pastor's

The Setting of Transformative Worship

schedule, the service can be led by lay people). Let the community decide which day and time works best for them. After six months to a year of experimenting, leaders can assess which services are serving the church's mission. This data will help them make an informed decision about the value of continuing to offer one service time over another and where to invest the congregation's energy to produce the desired result.[15]

Some congregations get excited about trying a second service but assume it should still be held on Sunday morning as the traditional day of Sabbath. The time for the second service is chosen so that the first service remains at the same time and becomes a kind of add-on in the attempt to numerically grow the congregation. Members will support it as long as it doesn't disrupt the status quo of the first service (and hence they make no effort to change). I have talked with many congregations who worship at 10:30 a.m. and offer other services at 8:30 a.m. or 12:00 p.m., but neither time attracts new people. Few congregations grow when members want to keep the worship time convenient for them and make the worship time inconvenient for seekers.[16] Disciples are willing to compromise to fulfill their mission to convert seekers to Christianity. After all, who wants to join a religious organization that makes people so inflexible and intolerant of change?

Again, I wish to emphasize that the times for worship should be based on the demographic of seekers and not on the guesswork or needs of the present membership. While an earlier service may appeal to some of the members, the premise isn't to make the time of worship more convenient for those who are already Christian. Before the church makes major changes to the forms of worship, it may be worth experimenting with the time of worship to see if the reason why people are not coming is because they work on Sunday morning. Also, if the neighborhood has an influx of workers during the week who return to their homes on the weekend, a worship service at lunch time or early Wednesday evening may peak their interest. Reaching seekers is usually not just about the time of worship.[17] If experimenting with multiple services does not reach seekers, the church will need to experiment with alternative forms of worship.

---

15. How many seekers convert to Christianity is an indicator of the church's success in its mission. I disagree with those who say it's not about the numbers and find that they speak out of frustration of not reaching seekers in the community.

16. These are not the best times for most people. Some people like the early hour but they do not tend to be young and few people want to worship at lunch time on Sunday.

17. Some congregations will latch on to this statement as a quick fix.

If the pastor anticipates a lot of resistance from the power brokers of the church and is not getting much support from the current membership, then a second worship service may be a better use of the pastor's energy.[18] This is the question: is it worth the pastor's energy to convince them to change the way they want to worship in the traditional service or is that energy better spent experimenting with alternative forms in a second service? I have known some pastors who were willing to take risks and try some really creative ways of worship in the attempt to reach seekers only to be criticized and condemned for these efforts. When this happens repeatedly, pastors become discouraged and may revert to people-pleasing. A second service can interject a renewed sense of energy not only for the pastor but for those members feeling the church is stagnant. Whenever a pastor calls me feeling deflated, defeated, and depressed, I suggest starting a second service (and they say "what?!").[19]

The issue of whether to invest energy into converting members to become disciples or to begin a second worship service (or more) has to do with the level of anticipated resistance by the current membership. Some pastors and leaders will feel so overwhelmed by a recent occurrence that they are not willing to take this on again. Other pastors fear the escalation of conflict to the point where they and their family will be the object of personal attacks. As a leader, I understand when it seems so much easier just to go with the current flow, even if that flow is in decline. It may seem counter to suggest investing energy into change, when to do so can be exhausting. In the attempt to help leaders to deal with resistance, I will add a chapter to this book. My intention is to equip the reader with practical ways of using resistance to bring about needed change.

---

18. It is better to fulfill half of the mission of converting seekers to Christianity. If the traditional worship service is not going to change to meet their religious needs, consider starting a second service. But remember, the pastor needs some disciples who are willing to form relationships and share stories so that seekers will be converted.

19. Breathing new energy into the dry bones of the pastor is one of the most effective ways of breathing new life into the dry bones of a congregation.

Chapter 10

Making Changes to Worship
Practical Ways to Deal with Resistance

CHANGE IS THE ESSENCE of life. Every creature on this planet has to learn to adapt to its changing environment. God created the world to balance consistency with the challenge of learning to deal with change. Organizations that shield people from this process by providing a haven where they can cling to the status quo do their members a disservice. By keeping everything the same as it was in 1955, the church has become a refuge from the forces of societal change. Advances in technology and science are not viewed as a gift for evangelism from the Creator but are frowned upon as a disruption to the continuity of what has always been and what members hope shall always be. While some churches enthusiastically use the latest technology to promote what they have to offer the community and continually assess if these services match what the community is looking for, others refuse to adapt, even if such resistance inevitably leads to closing the church.

Instead of functioning as a refuge from the shifts taking place in our culture, churches can be places that equip people to handle the changes happening in everyday life. Each of us experiences transitions as a natural aspect of living as a creature on this planet: the loss of a loved one or the loss of a job, relationship, or home. The church can help people to deal with these losses by studying the Bible and its gospel message to discern what God is doing through the process of grieving. These Christian practices equip individuals to adjust to their changing circumstances and develop empathy toward the suffering of others. As worshippers explore the teachings of Jesus, they are able to cope with sorrow and sadness, disappointment and frustration, and can face the future with hope for things to come.

They reflect the light of Christ for others as they live out the answer to the question, "What difference does being a Christian make in my life?"

A church (or a denomination) has less credibility to advocate for societal change if it is unwilling to assist individuals to change their lives (and change the organization itself to be conducive for this mission). Too frequently, the church's sole target for change is on those sustaining societal injustice. We are quick to note when oppression and prejudice negatively impact society but slower to confront the unequal distribution of power within our own organizations. The mainline denominational hierarchies continue to be mainly staffed by white men, early Boomers committed to maintaining the establishment. And yet, they can be deeply committed to marriage and economic equality and environmental preservation. Seekers do not want to participate in an organization that cannot see the need to remove the log from its own eye. They seek opportunities to change their lives by participating in making changes to society which, in turn, changes their lives.

I have presented several alternative forms of worship in this book. The reader may find some of them impractical, irrelevant, or even irreverent. Other ideas might get you excited but you think, "That would never work in my church!" As a pastor myself for twenty-five years, I have experimented with different ways to worship and most of them failed miserably.[1] Not every idea went over well with every member of every congregation. Resistance routinely arose by a group of people who were displeased whenever we introduced something new. We began to expect that when we made a change, someone would be upset and complain. Resistance indicates that a congregation is experiencing a change and thus, it is having an impact. When leaders respond with patience and perseverance (rather than trying to suppress their feelings), the potential exists for personal transformation as well.

In my work as a consultant, I have learned that every congregation has members who will resist change and when those members leave or pass on, another group will arise to take their place. Resistance is a systemic dynamic in the process of change. Those who resist are fulfilling a function that keeps the homeostasis (balance) of the organization. Without resistance, change would be so constant, it would wear out a congregation. It provides an internal timing mechanism for change: allowing for a phase of rest before taking on change again and so forth. It also demands space for feedback so that

---

1. I could write an entire book about everything I tried to numerically grow a congregation that didn't work. But out of all those attempts, I eventually found something that did produce the desired result. Keep trying!

changes are examined if they need to be tweaked to work more effectively and then evaluated for whether they produce the desired results. Resistance is also an expression of fear. Addressing these fears by helping members to identify and express them appropriately, helps them to imagine "the worst case scenario," which isn't as frightening as they might anticipate.[2]

Resistance is Energy

It takes a lot of energy to resist changes being made to a worship service. When congregations have no energy to resist, they may be suffering from congregational depression. A symptom of this condition is when members don't care what changes are made or whether they produce the intended effect. They make changes because they can't think of what else to do to get them out of their present predicament. They have lost hope and presume that any change is likely to fail. They may not make any changes for fear that the feeling of failure will worsen their organizational esteem and confidence. Depressed congregations cling blindly to the way they have always done things. Like depressed individuals, they think to themselves, "If we just do things the same way and veer neither to the right nor the left, we won't fall over the edge of the cliff into oblivion."

Resistance is a sign that a congregation is alive and well. For a congregation that has been depressed, resistance can signal that something is happening from within to alleviate their condition and access some energy. If leaders attempt to suppress that energy, they can inadvertently enable the congregation to become depressed again. Those who are attempting to create change may not be coming up with the best idea ever, but at least a few people are trying to help the congregation to move out of the dark hole. The question is not how do we reduce resistance, but how do we redirect that resistance toward efforts for change? How do we use the energy of resistance to get everyone on board and participate in its implementation? Suppressing resistance is a waste of energy, which could have been used to successfully reach the desired result.

As a form of energy, resistance is a neutral force with no value in and of itself. It is the way leaders respond to this energy that makes the difference concerning its impact.[3] When leaders attempt to get around it or squash it,

---

2. When members express fear about changing something, I ask, "What is the worst thing that could happen?"

3. Too often, leaders perceive resistance as a negative force to be navigated around.

they can enable its escalation to the level of conflict. Because conflict can be destructive, leaders themselves may fear resistance. But conflict can also be constructive when it provides an opportunity for members to change their lives: to learn how to deal with difference, address disagreement, and improve listening skills. Destructive conflict tolerates personal attacks, undermines channels of authority, and sabotages efforts from behind the scenes. Sadly, some congregations have a historical pattern of accessing energy by instigating conflict. When the latest controversy erupts, they become energized. They block any attempts to change as if the future of the church depends on their crusade of rightness.

When conflict is not confronted directly, it can escalate to a point where the congregation enables two or three people to hold the church hostage from moving forward. These people can be quite vocal in their opposition to the change being made. They use threats such as "this church will close" and "we won't be able to continue to pay the pastor" to raise the congregation's anxiety. They may threaten to withdraw their pledge and/or support for the pastor and/or their membership (and may even stop attending worship for a few weeks to make good on these threats). They may hold unsanctioned meetings in the parking lot or start an e-mail chain to instigate others. They may talk about "all the other people" who feel the same way they do but claim these people are too afraid to come forward. By exaggerating the extent of the resistance, their objective is to apply pressure on leaders to revoke the change.

Others may listen to them because they tend to be the ones who volunteer for everything. No one wants to lose their contribution or go against them, "because they do so much for the church!" This small group of members have exchanged volunteerism for power. They have given their time and talent under the assumption that they are deserving of a wider sway of influence than others. They may also prompt other members to be vocal on their behalf while they retreat into the background. If they can convince others of their rightness, they can sit back and watch the conflict unfold while they don't appear to be driving that conflict. By orchestrating resistance from behind the scenes, they can make it look more forceful and widespread. Underground conflict is more challenging to reconcile because leaders don't know where it is coming from and how many people are actually involved.[4]

---

4. What members should do is encourage disgruntle members to speak directly to the pastor, leaders, or to a pastor-parish relations team.

Making Changes to Worship

Thriving, Survival, and Panic Modes of Congregational Functioning

Congregations tend to function in one of three modes: thriving, survival, or panic. All three represent different forms of energy. Identifying which mode your congregation is currently functioning in gives leaders some understanding about how to introduce change and intervene when resistance develops.

What determines a thriving congregation has changed over the years. For the builder/silent generation, one criteria was a building project. There was excitement for the project, from the stages of planning to building the structure and celebrating its completion with a ribbon cutting ceremony. Houses were being built during the 1950s, creating suburban America. As a result, churches were filled to the brim. Many churches constructed educational wings to accommodate all the new children. To numerically grow a congregation, churches recited the mantra, "Build it and they will come." In a culture of obligation, when families were expected to attend worship, a brand-new facility to house a flourishing Christian education program for children and a "cool" room for the youth fellowship was all a church needed to fulfill its mission.

Today, the number of worshippers is not necessarily an indicator that a church is in thriving mode. It depends on which way the momentum is moving. For instance, if a church is numerically small but is increasing disciples each week, then they are likely thriving. These congregations know what they have to offer and what people are looking for. When they realize that what they have to offer is no longer what people want (religious needs change over time as cultural factors shift), they are willing to make changes to accommodate. They are open to new ways of worshipping with the hope of making disciples and furthering the mission of Jesus Christ. Thriving congregations believe that the church exists for the purpose of changing lives, not sustaining an outdated organizational structure or preserving "the way we have always done things."

When a congregation is thriving, members sense a good mood circulating. They encourage their leaders to experiment with new forms of worship. They may still be resistant to changes but there is a forum or grievance procedure for voicing one's opinion and members use these proper channels to do so. In thriving mode, they are receptive to change because, when changes have been made in the past, they have achieved the desired outcome (and if not, they were affirmed for their risk-taking, willingness to fail, and encouraged to try again). These results are observable and measurable. Members feel appreciated for their contribution. They believe that to serve the mission of the church is a means to serve God in Christ. When members have transitioned to disciples, there is less talk about their own likes and dislikes. It is more important to them to offer a variety of worship forms to meet the religious needs of a wider diversity of people.

In survival or panic mode, a congregation has tried making changes in the attempt to numerically grow but nothing is bringing seekers to worship. Members feel frustrated. "We've tried everything to attract new families, and they just don't want to come." They feel personally offended that others do not seem to want to worship the same way they do. The pastor is likely the motivator for change (and viewed as such by the members). He or she has attended workshops, read books like this, and suggested new ideas about how to grow the church. Members let him or her try these ideas, but because they offer little support, the ideas are like seeds that don't take root. The pastor becomes frustrated with the congregation and the congregation becomes frustrated with the pastor. One way to diagnosis if a congregation is in panic mode (and not just survival) is that they speak in "if-only" language. "If only we had a more competent pastor." "If only we had a younger pastor." "If only God would go *poof* and all the young families would come walking through the front door."[5]

Most mainline churches are currently functioning in survival mode: they have enough money so they don't feel a sense of urgency to have to make changes (and are often using their endowment to pay salaries, keep the heat on, and fund the basic necessities). They find little incentive to repurpose the church because "closing" is something that happens to other churches and can't possibly happen to them.[6] They may have a few young families attending, likely relatives of older members, and point to them as the "future" of the church (even though they participate in the present). The congregation may be on the verge of decline but members make assumptions about why this is happening and derive reasons beyond their control (e.g., the demographics of the neighborhood are shifting). They convince themselves that this is merely a phase in the church's history and when the neighborhood changes back, they will be in thriving mode once again.

---

5. Another prevalent one: "if only we had more money."

6. In my work I have found that congregations close not because they run out of money but because they run out of members.

Making Changes to Worship

In survival mode, there is a "freezing effect" around change. Members perceive that as long as they keep everything the same, they will survive. Change is seen as a threat to survival. Treading water in place (rather than swimming, as in thriving mode) appears to be the best strategy to keep the organization afloat. To do anything differently risks unintended (and unwanted) consequences. Resistance to change seems to protect their cherished church. Yet, the stagnancy of survival mode eventually wears some people out. (It takes energy to keep an organization static.) Some become overwhelmed by the threat of change while others become underwhelmed by the boredom of sameness. Once an organization functions in survival mode for several years, this way of functioning becomes the new normal. Members revert to making the purpose of church about their own wants and desires.

Survival and panic modes are often symptomatic of congregational depression. When a congregation has no energy to make changes, they likely have no energy to resist changes either. A new pastor may interpret this lack of resistance as support only later to be in a situation where they have accessed some energy to launch a campaign against him or her.[7] It doesn't take much for panic to set in and anxiety to surface (anxiety is a symptom of depression). When leaders respond by becoming anxious, they add to the anxiety and may be viewed as the source of these uncomfortable feelings.[8] "If we remove the pastor, then we remove the anxiety." Members' missional focus becomes reducing any anxiety in the attempt to return to a state of equilibrium. This regressive pull is so powerful and pervasive in an organization that once it works or at least reduces anxiety, it becomes the way in which they deal with any change.

A congregation that experiences a sudden change outside of their control (e.g., the pastor announces his or her retirement or resignation or they feel forced to face the fact that finances are dwindling), can easily slip from survival to panic mode. Panic is a form of anxiety that energizes people, and that energy can make people impulsive and mean-spirited, but it can also make them ready to accept the need for change. In panic mode, members become receptive as long as the leadership remains aware of their own anxiety (referred to as a "nonanxious presence").[9] This crisis presents

---

7. The pastor may respond, "Why am I only hearing these complaints now?"

8. When leaders begin to feel anxiety, they can help the congregation by identifying this feeling. They should also ask themselves, "Why am I feeling anxious at this time?"

9. Steinke, *Congregational Leadership*.

an opportunity for a congregation to assist members to learn how to more effectively cope with crises in their own lives.

Thus, thriving and panic are the two modes where members are receptive to change. In both modes the congregation can access energy. Although in panic mode that energy stems from anxiety (which may also be present in thriving mode but they are more aware of it). As long as leaders model how to manage that energy, it can be used to bring about positive change. In thriving mode, a congregation has learned new patterns to access energy that sustain changes for the long-term. The most challenging mode is survival, because the target of change is usually the organization itself, often at the expense of the individual. In survival mode, members may access energy through destructive conflict (e.g., members are energized to spread rumors but fail to follow through on tasks assigned to them in between committee meetings).

Practical Ways to Deal with Resistance

It has been my experience that the difference between constructive and destructive resistance is predetermined in the planning phase of change. When leaders clearly articulate the purpose of church and the function of worship, they build a foundation before constructing a house. That foundation is sturdy and the house withstands natural forces that threaten to blow it down. Otherwise, members ask, "Why are we doing this?" and assume these are efforts "to get new members" and "to get more money." A lack of vision, mission, and function is like a house built on quicksand. It's going to sink; it's just a matter of time. Destructive resistance sabotages all the hard work leaders do to make changes in the best interests of the organization. As much as everyone wants to jump to the forms of transformative worship, spending time and energy to prepare members by answering the "why" questions is effort well spent by the time the new forms of worship are being introduced.

One of the most effective ways of dealing with resistance is to encourage everyone to be involved throughout the process, from generating ideas to sustaining the change made. Often, resistance arises because some members, who expected and wanted to be asked to be involved, were overlooked as a source of support. They may not be angry about the change per se, but about the fact that they were not asked for their opinion or participation. What they object to is not being included. When they feel left out, perhaps even passed over in favor of some of the "newer" members of the church, they want to defend their previously held status in the church. They perceive the only option left to them is to assert their power by being resistant. To add fuel to the fire, if the change is affirmed as positive by the majority of members, they feel that newer members are saying that the way they have been worshipping is "wrong."

Instead of generating ideas in teams, as is often the case, ideas can be generated in congregational meetings. Then, teams are assigned tasks for their implementation. When the ideas begin to circulate among the congregation, everyone feels they have had a chance to express their opinion and offer to help. The premise of these meetings is not to get everyone to agree (which is only possible in a numerically small congregation that allows for centralized power), but to agree with the mission statement and a willingness to experiment with various ways of living into the mission. Consensus-building around an idea is a better way to get everyone involved than taking a vote so that some members win and others lose. Whenever this happens, the entire congregation loses resources, energy and support. By getting everyone on board from the beginning (even if they disagree with the change being made), leaders can direct energy toward a shared vision.

A congregation's vision is an image or pictorial representation of what they will look like as they live out their mission. Pastors need to give members a theological reason for engaging in the mission and when they don't, members will assume the church has chosen this mission because it needs the money. I have always found that when members perceive the changes being made are because God in Christ is calling them to reach a new demographic in their neighborhood, that they will go out of their way to do whatever is necessary to work toward this vision. When it's about making next year's budget, they are far less motivated to invite friends and family to worship. When a congregation has embraced a shared vision, framed in a theological message, members will practice discipleship by putting their beliefs into practice.

I refer to this aspect of the change process as the three C's of vision. The first is to *create* the vision. Hopefully, the chapter on assessing satisfaction levels provides leaders with a basis to determine which forms of worship are meeting the religious needs of the current membership and which are not. This exercise helps members realize everyone has religious needs and their needs are not all the same (and may be very different from the religious needs of seekers). Religious needs are subject to change when there is a shift of demographics in the church's neighborhood. A vision is how the church will look differently when worship embodies a diversity of people whose religious needs are being met, some of the time. Every member should be involved in creating this vision. The more people who participate in creating the vision, the less resistance will arise. Next, leaders *cast* the vision so that it will be *caught* and owned by the congregation. The wider the net for the vision to be cast, the more fish will be caught.

After the discernment process of current satisfaction levels, I suggest leaders discern "the nonnegotiables" by asking members, "What is most important to you about the way we worship? What change would be so out there that it would make you consider changing churches?" This should be part of the assessment process (described in chapter 4). Most members will not know how to answer these questions because they have not been asked. So they insist nothing changes, with a subconscious fear that what is most important to them will be sacrificed on the altar of church growth. When they feel as if the religious needs of others take priority over their own, they are likely to resist changes. By finding out what is most important to them (which, if they are being honest, is likely to be only one or two forms of worship and not the entire worship service), then they will be more willing to meet the religious needs of others.[10]

I also recommend developing "a behavioral covenant" before changes are made. This is a list of rules for engagement: the ways in which members are allowed to interact with one another and with the pastor. Individuals bring their dysfunction with them into congregational life, replaying dynamics from their family of origin, and their behavior can afflict the health of a congregation. Because the church is in the business of changing people's lives, we need to be able to clearly state appropriate patterns of relating and how we expect individuals to behave, especially when they are angry or frustrated. They are not allowed to come into a congregation and take power away from others, insist their needs be met above everyone else, or mistreat others. These rules should have consequences for trespassing so that members are held accountable for their actions. Too much dysfunction sabotages efforts to numerically grow a congregation, especially when everyone is afraid to confront those who are misbehaving.

---

10. It should be made clear that almost everything is on the table for potential change. Just because one or two members want to continue with certain forms and articulate so, doesn't mean that those forms won't change.

Making Changes to Worship

Grievance procedures inform members about the process if they have a complaint about worship, the pastor, another member, or the new color of paint in the sanctuary. Many churches do not make the procedure clear, for fear that to do so will prompt a lot of complaints by those who have held their tongue because they didn't know with whom to speak. Without making such a procedure well known, however, the church is inadvertently enabling parking-lot conversations. Resistance may be ignited from secret meetings so that by the time the leadership recognizes there is a problem, it has become a burning fire of conflict. A complaint should first be brought to the attention of the pastor (even if the complaint is about the pastor), as this gives the pastor the opportunity to respond and provide pastoral care (which is what may really be needed). If this does not suffice, the person can bring a complaint to the appropriate committee or team (e.g., pastoral relations, deacons, or church council). Most complaints about changes to the worship service could be handled effectively if members knew how to go about voicing them.

After the worship team has been empowered by the congregation to experiment with new forms over the next several weeks, they should announce these changes to give the congregation time to prepare. If members do not anticipate the change, it may feel forced upon them and they will respond with resistance.[11] Pastors should remind the congregation that they have prayed together, assessed the current satisfaction levels, and discerned that God is calling them to do things differently to fulfill their mission. Leaders also need to be sensitive to members' feelings about change and provide empathy. A statement by the pastor the week before the change is being made can go a long way to unifying the congregation: "We realize that some of you may not like this kind of music and perhaps it even makes you feel uncomfortable. But you told us you want to do a better job reaching our neighbors, and surveys show that this kind of music is likely to meet their religious needs to worship God."

I suggest making small changes initially. This gives the church time to adjust to the rocking motion of the boat and feel confident that they will not tip over. Small changes that produce results demonstrate to the congregation that we can do this, which accesses energy and builds momentum. Some members need to be reassured that if the church makes changes to worship,

---

11. Members either say, "We are making this happen" or "this is happening to us." The difference is between the active and passive voice. When they speak in the passive voice, they are more likely to resist changes.

the steeple will not fall down. Small changes should be instituted at a gradual pace with intervals in-between to give the system a chance to stabilize. This may frustrate some members, especially those who feel a sense of urgency, while others will feel overwhelmed. There is usually a significant number of members sitting by the sidelines watching to see what is going to happen before they are willing to get into the game. If the small changes produce a desired outcome and the majority of the congregation support these changes, then they will get on board, but if the flow seems to be moving in the opposite direction (i.e., resistance), they will support that direction.

Changes can be implemented in degrees of impact. I refer to small changes as the 2X phase in which a current form of worship is tweaked. For example, instead of the pastor doing the welcome, a member of the congregation does a welcome and answers the question, "Why do I attend this church?" Members will probably like these changes and if so, leaders can move to the next phase of moderate change, which has a 5X factor. Examples of moderate change are offering small groups during worship, changing the culture of being silent during worship and not talking to asking questions during the sermon, or shifting the music from the organ to instrumentalists while getting worshippers up to dance. Moderate change introduces new forms of worship and subtracts other forms which are no longer working toward the mission. Moderate change involves a leap of faith and needs longer intervals in between than the 2X phase to provide a period of respite in between changes made.

High-impact change has a 10X factor. It will feel huge. An example is selling the building because seekers are leaving the community and purchasing or renting another building where they are moving. High-impact changes should be prayerfully considered over a significant period of time so that everyone is on board. Hopefully, the change is being made to do the work of Jesus Christ and not because the congregation feels forced and out of options. Some congregations will not need to make high-impact changes (as the small and moderate changes will produce the desired results), but this option should be contemplated when the congregation believes this is what God wants them to do. Too often, moderate change brings in few new people (small changes usually only prepares the congregation for new people), and the church readjusts, the boat stops rocking, and they stop there. High-impact change should always be on the horizon as a possibility if small and moderate changes do not help the congregation to fulfill their mission.

Making Changes to Worship

I am also often asked at what point should we make changes to the way we worship: before seekers come, while they are coming, or after they come? Most congregations think they should wait until the new people come because these changes do not meet the religious needs of the current membership. Waiting until they come risks that those who find their way into a worship service are not likely return a second Sunday. It doesn't matter if a promise is made that changes will happen if they return (e.g., "We will begin an educational program for your children if you come back"). Disciples need to be prepared for their arrival. After they start coming, they will also have their own ideas about the way that they want to worship and hope that the congregation will be open to them. If they say, "Oh, we just love everything about the way this church worships," you should anticipate that it will only be a matter of time before they voice their own needs and/or simply stop attending (more likely). Changes should be made before, during, and after seekers come to a worship service.

When I begin consulting with congregations, I ask, what are you afraid that I am going to say or suggest? They are afraid I am going to make them change everything about the worship service (as if I have that much power!) and they won't like the changes. They fear I will tell them everything they have always done has been "wrong" and understandably, they feel defensive. Some hope I remembered to bring my magic wand and will wave it over the community who will suddenly appear at the front door of the church and want to worship the same way they have always worshipped. They fear that I am going to ask them to sacrifice their own religious needs 100 percent in favor of meeting 100 percent of the religious needs of those who have not yet set foot in their church. I reassure them that discipleship is always about transforming the disciple first (just like Jesus did) and then the spiritual seeker.

Long-term members also need space to grieve; not necessarily the glory days of the past, but the hope in 1955 of what they anticipated church life would be like in their elder years. They expected young people would come and take over the work of the church as they aged and could no longer do it. Now they find themselves still working in the church just to keep it afloat. They had high hopes of what the church could do in the world to transform society and resolve contemporary social problems but now it seems as if the church has become just another declining organization, disconnected from its community and seemingly irrelevant in its message. Before we move forward to implement transformative worship to attract all generations to the church, a good cry will serve us well. It didn't happen the way we expected: but maybe as a Christian community we should believe it is working out the way God in Christ intends as we build the Kingdom here on earth.

Concluding Reflections

The sun rises, the birds sing, and the stone is rolled away. We are a resurrection people. We can only move forward to be the church God calls us to be for the future. By letting go of that which is no longer meeting the religious needs of members and seekers alike, we become responsive to the work of the Holy Spirit creating something fresh and wonderful, inspirational and innovative. I hope and pray that readers will be able to explore options and imagine new possibilities to envision their church filled with people in the pews once again with a joyful spirit in their midst. Children run up and down the aisles and people smile because they remember there was a time in our history when there were no children in worship. The youth are gathered in the balcony, laughing and talking and not really paying attention to the worship leader, but when the musicians start playing music that appeals to them, they are engaged and excited to be in worship.

A new day is dawning in the emerging church. The forms we have used worked well to meet the needs of past generations but are not meeting the needs of the present, and likely will not meet those of future generations. It is not just a matter of making changes to attract new people, but becoming clear about why we do what we do when we gather together. In 1955, babies were converted to Christianity by baptism, but today we seek to convert adults who have not grown up attending church. Therefore, we need new forms of worship to meet their religious needs. And when members take this mission to heart, when they believe that Christ himself is commissioning them to do this work, then they will put their beliefs into practice and in so doing, find that their own lives have been changed.

Bibliography

Baskette, Molly Phinney. *Standing Naked Before God: The Art of Public Confession.* Cleveland: Pilgrim, 2015.
Bowers, Laurene Beth. *Becoming a Multicultural Church.* Cleveland: Pilgrim, 2006.
———. *Designing Contemporary Congregations: Strategies to Attract Those Under Fifty.* Cleveland: Pilgrim, 2008.
———. *The God Beyond Organized Religion.* Eugene, OR: Wipf & Stock, 2016.
———. *Invitational Ministry: Move Your Church from Membership to Discipleship.* St. Louis: Chalice Press, 2014.
Butler-Bass, Diana. *Christianity for the Rest of Us: How the Neighborhood Church is Transforming the Faith.* San Francisco: HarperSanFrancisco, 2006.
Crabtree, J. Russell. *Owl Sight: Evidence-Based Discernment and the Promise of Organizational Intelligence for Ministry.* Saint John, NB: Magi Press, 2012.
Froese, Paul, and Christopher Bader. *America's Four Gods: What We Say About God—and What That Says About Us.* Oxford: Oxford University Press, 2010.
James, William. *The Varieties of Religious Experience: A Study in Human Nature.* New York: Penguin Classics, 1990.
McFee, Marcia. *The Worship Workshop: Creative Ways to Design Worship.* Nashville: Abingdon, 2002.
Nierenberg, Roger. *Maestro: A Surprising Story About Leading by Listening.* New York: Penguin, 2009.
Putman, Robert D. *Bowling Alone: The Collapse and Revival of American Community.* New York: Simon & Schuster, 2000.
Putman, Robert D., and David E. Campbell. *American Grace: How Religion Divides and Unites Us.* New York: Simon & Schuster, 2010.
Reese, Martha Grace. *Unbinding the Gospel: Real Life Evangelism.* St. Louis: Chalice Press, 2008.
Steinke, Peter. *Congregational Leadership in Anxious Times: Being Calm and Courageous No Matter What.* Lanham, MD: Rowman & Littlefield, 2006.
Sweet, Leonard. *The Gospel According to Starbucks: Living With a Grande Passion.* Colorado Springs: Waterbrook, 2007.
Thiel, Peter. *From Zero to One: Notes on Startups, or How to Build the Future.* New York: Crown Business, 2014.
Tickle, Phyllis. *The Great Emergence: How Christianity is Changing and Why.* Grand Rapids: Baker Books, 2012.

www.ingramcontent.com/pod-product-compliance
Lightning Source LLC
Chambersburg PA
CBHW071434160426
43195CB00013B/1899